IN BEAUJOLAIS

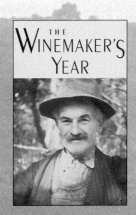

THE WINEMAKER'S YEAR

IN BEAUJOLAIS

by Michael Buller ❖ photographs by Pierre Cottin ❖ preface by Paul Bocuse & Gerard Canard

THAMES AND HUDSON

First published in the United States in 1993 by
Thames and Hudson Inc., 500 Fifth Avenue,
New York, New York 10110

First published in Great Britain in 1993 by
Thames and Hudson Ltd, London

Library of Congress Catalog Card Number 93-60254

British Library Cataloguing-in-Publication Data
A catalogue record for this book is available
from the British Library
ISBN 0-500-01584-8

Art directed and designed by
Beth Tondreau Design
Printed and bound in Singapore

My thanks, for their encouragement: Peter MF Sichel; Hugh Johnson; Frank Prial; Michael Aaron, Sherry Lehmann; André Soltner; Alexis Lichine; Doris Tobias; Mary Mulligan, International Wine Center; Alexis Bespaloff; Eunice Fried; Harriet and Bill Lembeck; Joshua Wesson; David Rosengarten; Abdullah Simon; Paul Kovi and Tom Margittai, Four Seasons; William Deutsch; Gerard Yvernault; Ed Lauber; Julius Wile; Ferdinand Metz, Culinary Institute of America; Jules Epstein; Kevin Zraly; Ray Wellington; Millard Cohen; Peter Lorcker; Ellen Alexander; Peter Sheahan; Dorothy Cann, French Culinary Institute; Grace and Deborah Kent; Kathleen Talbert; Bobbe Seigel; Ursula Viet; Boris Hoffman; Carol Rothman, McGinn-Cazale Theater; Julian Granirer; Ronald and Monica Searle; Jacques Esterel; Frank Dunlop; Dan Sturge-Moore, Radio-Diffusion-Télévision-Française; Georges Brassens; René Fallet; Jacques Brel; Catherine Rouvel; Jean Rouvet; Jacques Canetti; Christian Millau; Henri Gault; Michel Bourdeaux, The Vatel Club; André Jammet, La Caravelle; Alain Querre, Château Monbousquet, St. Emilion; Jeanne-Marie Perry and Stacy Ackerman, Thames and Hudson, New York; Bill Rusin, W. W. Norton; Amy Donaldson.

To

HENRI DE RAMBUTEAU

*whose great love of Beaujolais
runs through this story*

My thanks to my friend, photographer Pierre Cottin, whose caring, loving work on Beaujolais over the years gave me these dramatic images; and photographer Patrick Perche, born and bred in Beaujolais, who worked with me, contributing exciting new material in the last weeks.

And to three major players in Beaujolais: Henri de Rambuteau, who believed and gave me so much of himself over twenty years; Gerard Canard, who with kindness, warmth and understanding has been the longstanding guardian angel of this work; and Paul Bocuse, Chef of the Century and leader on both sides of the Atlantic, who has been a true friend. Grands mercis.

My sincerest thanks and respect for the vision and warm encouragement of Peter Warner, President of Thames and Hudson, New York, who steadily made my first and now my second book possible. My deep thanks to Beth Tondreau, who breathes life, shape, and depth each time into the layout of these books. And to all at Thames and Hudson in New York and London.

A special place for playwright Jeannie Rowan, my wife, whose critiques, fine editing, and company through Beaujolais country in the final stages of the book was what I dearly needed.

Contents

Preface

❖ BY ❖

PAUL BOCUSE

M y father was a cook, my grandfather was a cook, and we are a family of cooks who have lived in our village of Collanges-au-Mont d'Or, just outside Lyon, since 1635. We are deeply attached to our country and to the river, the Saône, that runs by.

We are closely attached to our vineyards, too. Every year after the harvest, in December or January, my father and I went to buy our Beaujolais for the restaurant. The buying of our Beaujolais was always important. We would buy for the whole year, in barrels of 215 liters. We would spend one or two days visiting the winegrowers and tasting with them. It was always an occasion for celebration and eating, and of course the Beaujolais had pride of place. They say that Lyon has three rivers: the Saône, the Rhône, and the Beaujolais.

The seasons are important for the chef and the winegrower. I see the leaves falling in autumn, and shortly thereafter the new wine, the Beaujolais Nouveau, arrives. In spring, when I see cherry trees in bloom, the mature Beaujolais of the year arrives in bottles and is brought to the table. We change our menus four times a year according to the seasons and depending on the produce we find in the region.

I have made many lifetime friends among the winegrowers and *négociants,*

or merchants, of Beaujolais. They come and sit at my table here in the restaurant. I visit them, walk with them in their vineyards, taste with them in their cellars. Every year we celebrate the *grand départ,* the departure, of the New Wine. Today I have my own vineyard in the Beaujolais.

Michael Buller has been coming to my restaurant since 1974 when my colleague Jean Troisgros called me one day to say Michael was on his way over for dinner. On his visits, Michael accompanies me to the market, joins me at my table, and visits my friends in Beaujolais.

From his years in the cellars with the winegrowers and *négociants,* he has brought back this marvelous story that is their story, word for word. He listens and understands. As recorder of the oral history of our region, he has been an ambassador and friend.

May I recommend a bottle of Beaujolais and, with your friends, fill the glasses all around, open this book and read on. Share this warm, satisfying journey through our region of France. *Bon appétit* and *bon voyage!*

— PAUL BOCUSE

Preface

❖ BY ❖

GERARD CANARD

For more than thirty years, my work has been to sing the praises of the sense of conviviality that makes Beaujolais a wine unlike any other wine. It is a reputation that comes as much from our winegrowers' annual search for quality as from the chain we forge of good companions around the world.

With my colleague the late Comte Henri de Rambuteau, my predecessor as president of the Confrérie des Compagnons du Beaujolais, we set out in 1971 to the United States with our Beaujolais as one of the flagships of the wines of France. Henri was elected our official ambassador. Michael Buller, already over there, was our guide.

It was therefore right and natural that when Michael came to Beaujolais we should be his guides. We are 9500 winegrowers of Beaujolais, Beaujolais-Villages, and ten Beaujolais Growths, and some forty *négociants* of Beaujolais. We work seriously, yet without taking ourselves too seriously, to make wine from a grape born of a common father, the black Gamay of white juice, that succeeds nowhere so well as here on our Beaujolais soil.

I believe our wine is inimitable, so nothing can stop me from telling you the secret of its success. Better still, Michael invites you to a unique *assemblage* of promenades over the years through our towns and villages, châteaux

and simple *domaines,* cellars and vineyards. He tells the story of our men and women of Beaujolais in their own words.

On Michael's first day here, Henri in his usual gentle, friendly way told him, "Look into your glass and see the harmony of our hillsides, the smile of the winegrower's wife, the charm of our ancient sites, vineyards, and cellars."

From the depths of cellars, Michael has recorded these confidences of the winegrowers—fascinating in their country wisdom and courage, in their ties to the soil, in their *joie de vivre.* As an old winegrower told Michael one evening after they had tasted his wines, "The Good Lord, who knows me well, appeared in a dream the other night and said, 'Drink your wine while you're on earth. I don't have anything like it up here.'"

I salute the wine of my little Beaujolais country, endowed with such sweet-smelling charm, such joy and fruit from the soil, so full-bodied and light from the sunshine. I salute our winegrowers, whose major claim to fame is that through this most spiritual of wines they have added gaiety to our countryside, colored the imagination of its inhabitants, and learned how to share this with the world, with the help of such fine ambassadors as Michael Buller.

— GERARD CANARD
Directeur, Union Interprofessionnelle des Vins du Beaujolais
Président, Confrérie des Compagnons du Beaujolais

THE CHÂTEAU OWNER'S STORY

My first visit to Beaujolais country, over twenty years ago, took me down Route Nationale 6 that runs south from Paris, the old coach road leading through Fontainebleau to Lyon and eventually on down to the Mediterranean. You could also travel on the romantic-sounding Train Bleu from Paris, replaced today by the streamlined TGV, *train de grande vitesse,* which takes a little over an hour to reach Mâcon just north of Beaujolais. The new and unromantic autoroute is a poor alternative to the old coach road that provides one with a dramatic experience: as you reach a desolate plateau called Le Morvan and start down a long steep hill past the village and château named Le Rochepot, the nostrils fill with the warm air of Provence, and you can imagine the blue of the Mediterranean four hundred miles south as the birds fly.

Follow the valley of the river Saône through the southern Burgundy and Mâcon wine regions to the stretch of road between the towns Belleville and Villefranche. If you take any of the small roads and lanes to the right, they will lead you into Beaujolais country. I usually head for what the wine writer Frank Prial calls "a wide part in the road," the village of Le Breuil in southern Beaujolais, and the eighteenth-century Château des Granges.

Comte Henri de Rambuteau is the owner, or *proprietaire,* of the château that, apart from a clock tower dating from the twelfth century, is largely eighteenth-century, restored by the Lombard branch of Henri's family at the turn of this century. "I have an acre of tiles to keep in good repair," Henri told me as we walked around. "I need to increase my wine sales so I can get the château roof fixed."

Henri began working not in wine but in the textile business in Lyon. The textile business had been flourishing since the seventeenth century and had built Lyon into the second city of France. The silks, taffetas, velvets, and satins manufactured in Lyon furnished royal palaces from Versailles to St. Petersburg, filling the salons and wardrobes of Marie Antoinette, Madame de Pompadour, Josephine Bonaparte, and Catherine of Russia. The houses of Lyon, such as Bianchini-Ferier, Bucol, rivaled Milan with their fine fabrics for fashion. The advent of synthetic fibers caused a sad decline in the textile business in Lyon, and Henri retired to his family property to tend his vines. He traveled now as ambassador for the Beaujolais winegrowers. Tall, upright, plain-spoken with excellent English, he described himself: "I sound like Maurice Chevalier or Charles Boyer, depending on my audience."

After lunch on a fine autumn day, my host walked me around the property. "I have sixty acres of vineyard, enormous for this part of the Beaujolais. There are four vineyards around here." He pointed. "See those vines, as fine as you'll find anywhere. They belong to a neighbor, an excellent winemaker. And on the other side there's a family of four brothers, real workers, who sometimes experiment but never take risks. A third vineyard belongs to a man who went to agricultural college in Montpellier and learned many things. He believes, in my opinion, that he's learned much more than he really has. Infused with science, all he does is experiment. He thinks he's going to discover everything. I don't think it brings him much money.

"From my vineyard I'll get about eighty or ninety hectoliters per hectare this year. I could send workers out to remove one of every two grapes, they're so heavily clustered, but what if it hails? Another vineyard I planted will be ripe much earlier, suggesting we're in for a cold period. Cold and humidity near harvesttime precedes a warming-up in the weather that means risk of rot. We never know what to expect. Here comes my neighbor, one of the brothers."

"Bonjour, monsieur le comte."

"Bonjour, monsieur, did the hail damage your grapes?"

"About fifteen percent, like last year, but this time the grapes are larger."

"Larger and ripe. As long as it doesn't rain as well."

The neighbor nodded and went about his work. Henri looked at the sky across the hills ahead. "Since the Beaujolais is where the winds of the Atlantic and Loire River valley meet the winds coming up the Rhône River valley from the Mediterranean, it hails often. These hills were the sites for a signal system under the Gauls. The capture of Rome by the Gauls was known in the north of France within two days. During the French Revolution the same system of signal fires was used. If the sky was clear with no fog or mists, messages went faster than by horse."

I set off with Henri on my first tour of the Beaujolais region. He was an ideal companion, with words and gestures as big and warm and full of life as the wine he made.

"We'll take the road to Vaux," he said as he drove, "the village famous as the setting for a celebrated novel of the thirties, *Clochemerle* by Gabriel Chevalier. Every village in Beaujolais is Clochemerle. I often say to my wife that some of the incidents and characters in our village Le Breuil are straight out of *Clochemerle.* We have one winegrower who lives near us, a lady noted for her rather large mouth. One day at a luncheon in our village, I was seated next to her and she began, 'Monsieur, what is your job?'

"'Mademoiselle, I'm an agricultural worker. I have vines.'

"'You mean there are vines around here?'

"'Listen, mademoiselle. Around here we respect the vine. We reserve for it the best soils and the best places. We are not like some regions in Beaujolais where there are vines anywhere that vines can be made to grow—vines in the cemeteries, vines in the curate's garden, vines even along the roadside.' Since that described her region, I had peace for the rest of the meal."

Outside the next village, Henri pulled up alongside a man.

"*Bonjour, monsieur le maire,*" they greeted each other, since they were mayors of their respective towns.

"I'm showing the Beaujolais to my friend Michel," said Henri. "We don't owe him any money but we do owe him several *canons* of Beaujolais."

One hour and several *canons* later, Henri is at the wheel again, explaining, "Beaujolais is divided into two parts: lower or Bas-Beaujolais where I live, and upper or Haut-Beaujolais, with its nine Growths or *Crus:* Saint-Amour, Chiroubles, Fleurie, Moulin-à-Vent, Morgon, Brouilly, Côtes de Brouilly, Chenas, and Juliénas.** You may have your own opinion as to which is the best; I think the rating should change every year.

"Moulin-à-Vent is generally considered our top Beaujolais. Though they make their wine from the same grapes as ours, there is manganese in their soil which gives it a special taste. During the First World War there was a shortage of manganese, so they checked geological maps and discovered that they could mine it in the *Appellation Contrôlée* region of Moulin-à-Vent.

"Morgon is usually the hardest wine of them all. We say around here, when we're checking our vats of wine, 'That wine *morgonne!*' meaning it has the characteristics of a Morgon. I find that the lightest, most typical Beaujolais comes from the Chiroubles and Fleurie. In Saint-Amour, which is the most northerly and borders the Mâcon region of Burgundy, one goes from red to white wines within a matter of twenty meters—a little white Beaujolais that slightly resembles the white Mâcon wine of Saint-Veran.

"Here in the south we produce plain Beaujolais, theoretically one degree less minimum strength of alcohol than Beaujolais-Villages. Our soil is clay-limestone. As for Beaujolais-Supérieur, forget it. My wines could be called Beaujolais-Supérieur as my vineyards are on higher ground and supposedly better. But it's unfair and meaningless, so I stopped using the word *Supérieur.*

"The wines in the Growths' regions have to be pruned in *gobelet;* not on wires as we're allowed. They're limited to 356 gallons per acre, whereas we're allowed 445 per acre."

....

**In 1989, a tenth Beaujolais Cru was added, Regnié.

The Beaujolais Wine Map:
Beaujolais, Beaujolais-Villages, and the Beaujolais Crus

Beaujolais: Average annual production: 35,000,000 gallons (1,300,000 hectoliters)

50% Beaujolais, 25% Beaujolais Villages, 25% Crus

50% of the annual production is exported

Beaujolais
16,000,000 gallons (608,000 hectoliters)
24,000 acres (9,700 hectares)

Beaujolais-Villages
10,000,000 gallons (360,000 hectoliters)
15,500 acres (5,850 hectares)
Beaujolais Nouveau (Beaujolais and Beaujolais-Villages) represents 30% of the region's total annual production.

Beaujolais Crus

Moulin-à-Vent

9,000 gallons (34,000 hectoliters)

1,595 acres (646 hectares):

    825 acres (334 hectares) in the commune

        of Romanéche-Thorins (Saône-et-Loire)

    770 acres (312 hectares) in the

    commune of Chenas (Rhône)

Fleurie

1,200,000 gallons (45,000 hectoliters)

1,958 acres (793 hectares) in the commune of Fleurie

Brouilly

1,900,000 gallons (72,000 hectoliters)

3,000 acres (1,215 hectares):

    889 acres (360 hectares)

    in the commune of Odenas

    765 acres (310 hectares) in the commune of St. Lager

    370 acres (150 hectares) in the commune of Cercié

    346 acres (140 hectares) in the

    commune of Quincie (Rhône)

    321 acres (130 hectares) in the commune of Charentay

    309 acres (125 hectares) in the

    commune of St.-Etienne-La-Varenne

Beaujolais

Beaujolais-Villages

Brouilly

Côtes de Brouilly

Lyon

LYON •

Régnié   Morgon   Chiroubles   Fleurie   Moulin-à-Vent   Chénas   Juliénas   Saint-Amour

Paris

W
S ← → N
E

Côte de Brouilly

450,000 gallons (17,000 hectoliters)

703 acres (258 hectares):

    284 acres (115 hectares) in the
        commune of Odenas

    321 acres (130 hectares) in St. Lager

    49 acres (20 hectares) in Cercié

    49 acres (20 hectares) in Quincie (Rhône)

Chiroubles

500,000 gallons (19,000 hectoliters)

    854 acres (346 hectares) in the
        commune of Chiroubles (Rhône)

Chenas

370,000 gallons (14,000 hectoliters)

637 acres (257 hectares):

    412 acres (166 hectares) in
        la Chapelle-de-Guinchay (Saône-et-Loire)

    225 acres (91 hectares) in Chenas (Rhône)

Beaujolais-Villages

10,000,000 gallons (360,000 hectoliters)

15,500 acres (5,850 hectares)

Beaujolais Nouveau (Beaujolais and Beaujolais-Villages)
represents 30% of the region's total annual production.

Juliénas

850,000 gallons (32,000 hectoliters)

1,420 acres (575 hectares):

> 1,037 acres (420 hectares) in Juliénas (Rhône)
>
> 197 acres (80 hectares) in Jullié (Rhône)
>
> 185 acres (75 hectares) in Pruzilly
> (Saône-et-Loire)
>
> 1.2 acres (0.5 hectares) in Emeringes (Rhône)

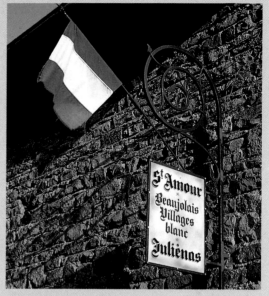

Morgon

1,600,000 gallons (61,000 hectoliters)

2,650 acres (1,073 hectares) in the commune of
Villié-Morgon

Regnié

950,000 gallons (36,000 hectoliters)

1,482 acres (600 hectares) in the commune of
Regnié-Durette (Rhône)

Saint-Amour

450,000 gallons (17,000 hectoliters)

696 acres (282 hectares) in Saint-Amour
(Saône-et-Loire)

Total Beaujolais production
includes 290,000 gallons
(11,000 hectoliters) of white
Beaujolais

Henri appeared most concerned about the prospects for his family, four sons and a daughter. One of the sons would one day take over the management of the vineyards and cellars from Henri. "When we speak of prosperity for the Beaujolais winegrowers, it is quite recent and very fragile. Their parents worked the vineyards and, as was the thing to do, later bought land and set up for themselves. Then came the hard years: vineyards largely abandoned, the young men leaving. Beaujolais was dying of hunger. Now the winegrowers' children don't have to take up the plow or dig as hard as their parents. They're happy to stay and help. Personally I don't think the young should go to agricultural colleges; all they learn is how to become agricultural specialists with theories on soils and different pesticides. I prefer my sons to learn something about commerce and the wine trade, so they will understand amortization, profits, and losses."

....

Henri had a deep sense of family and history. He saw it everywhere about him. He told the history of France like a storyteller of ages past. We stopped on a hill, Mont Tourvéon near Chenelette, with a sweeping view of the Beaujolais regions. "History has it that Emperor Charlemagne sent his son Charles to capture the château on this hill. Ganelon the Traitor, who sent Charlemagne's army to its death in the Pass of Roncevalles in Spain, was captured here, placed in a barrel, and rolled from the top of the hill to the bottom. What remained inside the barrel was little more than a hamburger. At the spot where the hamburger stopped, they built a church here at Chenelette that has a peculiarity: it stands outside its village.

"The valley of the Saône and beyond are the marshes and flats of a low-lying land called Les Dombes. We are on the road to Lyon, once the main road from Rome to Cluny, when the Abbey of Cluny was a great center of learning."

We descended into the valley, to a town of gray stone houses that reminded me of a Welsh mining town. Henri drove to a friend's cellar, where he announced, glass in hand, "Welcome to the first capital of Beaujolais, Beaujeu. It gave its name to the wine. We are on the old Beaujolais Road, built in the reign of Louis XIV. Before then, Beaujolais never left the region, it was drunk

at Lyon or in the cafés around. Thanks to this road, the wine left on carts pulled by horses or oxen over the hills until it reached the Loire at Charlieu; then by boat to Gien just below Orléans and then by canal to Paris. To take it all the way to Paris by road through Burgundy would have been very long and expensive, especially since the Burgundy towns of Mâcon and Dijon levied heavy taxes on wines from the south, to protect their own wines which were also being sent up to Paris.

"One hadn't the right to take the wine beyond Beaujeu without having a bar of wood fixed across the top of the barrel. Just above Beaujeu is the little village of Les Dépôts where the convoys would stop and strong men called *barreurs* would remove the barrels from the carts, draw off some ten liters of wine from each barrel, close it up again, and put on the bar. The tighter they got the metal bands around the barrel, the less room there was for the wine. What remained was therefore theirs to drink." He raised his glass and nodded thanks to his friend. "They still say around here, 'He drinks like a *barreur.*'"

··········

On the way back from Beaujeu, in Villefranche, the modern capital of the Beaujolais region, we called in at the bistro opposite the offices of the winegrowers' union, a bar known among winegrowers as the Annexe where for twenty years I have always found a group of Beaujolais leaders seated around their *canons* at the end of the day. "All our major decisions are taken here," I was told by Gerard Canard, director of the union since its inception in 1959. The first time I visited the Annexe, they were all planning the annual visit from Paris by the Académie Rabelais.

Henri explained how the Académie had been founded in Lyon during the Second World War, Lyon being the home for a time of some of France's food journalists. "The principal distraction and drink was the Beaujolais. France's famous satirical weekly, *Le Canard Enchaîné,* was our great promoter in the paper's early days. Especially since two of its leading writers come from the Beaujolais; one from my next-door village, Le Bois d'Oignt."

··········

Henri had been mayor of Le Breuil and its 460 inhabitants for the past twenty years. "When my children went to the village school and were asked what was the capital of France, they would always cry, 'Le Breuil!' Our village is Catholic, rare in Beaujolais, and Sunday morning there's Mass at nine. When Mass is over, everyone gathers outside on the square to talk, mostly about the weather."

He took me to his mayoral office, where he sat down at his desk, puffing at his pipe. "After Mass, from ten till midday here under the bust of Marianne, I hold my meeting of village councillors, I listen to their complaints, usually neighbors' stories, sometimes very funny. My assistant mayor always leaves at the beginning of the meeting, saying he has to fetch the bread. Actually he goes to the bistro opposite, where he's president of the local bowling club, the most thriving sporting activity in the village. At eleven forty-five he returns, making a lot of noise, asking questions about what's been going on. Then he begins to get thirsty, starts walking round and round the room announcing it's time to go and drink a *canon* of Beaujolais. So we walk across to the bistro and find half the village; they've been there since Mass. All the men, that is, since the women never go to the bistro. As soon as I arrive I hear questions like 'Are you going to increase taxes, *monsieur le maire?*'"

....

Henri took great pride in his pressing house, a vast barn with tall wooden doors that creaked open unsteadily. Opposite the vats stood a massive wooden construction that reached almost up to the rafters. "That's my great winepress. You see it has carved on it *Pair de France,* an honorary title bestowed under the monarchy after the Empire, between 1815 and 1830. *Pair* is the equivalent of a lord in England. My great-grandfather was so proud to be made Pair de France that he had it carved everywhere—all over the house. It meant more to him than the Légion d'Honneur. So I know the press dates pre-1830. The other press over there we've used for at least fifty years. Last spring my workers said to me:

"'We can't go on working this press, monsieur.'

"'Why not?' I asked them.

"'Because, monsieur, it's too old. It's prehistoric.'

" 'Listen, my father bought it the year I was born.'

" 'Precisely, monsieur, that's why we say it's old.'

"So I had to buy a new press."

·········

Before dinner, we turned the pages of the family photo album. "That's my vineyard foreman, *Monsieur le Préfet* as we call him. A tough guy to handle, very bright. Last week we didn't quite agree. Out in the forest cutting down my trees, I wanted certain trees cut, so finally I asked him, 'Who's going to decide?' Without hesitation, he replied, 'Me. I've been working longer than you for the family. Your father appointed me foreman two years before you were born.' I had to give in.

Sutorius Bourricand, édit. Bois-d'Oingt
Ouvrage du Château de RAMBUTEAU pres le Bois-d'Oingt (Rhône)

"Another day in the forest with him and his son, cutting down trees, it was extremely cold with snow on the ground. He was standing there, his hands in his trouser pockets, unable to move with cold. 'Can I lend you some gloves, *Monsieur le Préfet?*' I asked. He replied, 'Monsieur, because it's Sunday and because of your visit, I'm wearing my longjohns. I'm not accustomed to them and they don't fit me. So if you don't object, I'll get rid of them.' Right there in the forest, he proceeded to drop his trousers, step out of his longjohns, and hang them on the branch of a tree. Then he pulled up his trousers and started to work again."

Twice a day, lunch and dinner, the Rambuteau family assembled at the long table in the kitchen, a bench down either side. On fine days like today, the door was left open for the last rays of the sun to enter and reflect in the copper pans hung high along the wood-paneled walls. They all had their place, including Adrien the cellar handyman. Henri's wife, Irline, sat at the head of the table. The children at the table had grown up with their father's oral history of France, the region, and the village.

He brought to the table a bottle without label or cork of his own wine. "We drink Beaujolais as new as possible. The best wine is the wine in the vat, so I never bottle any of the Beaujolais I drink in my home. We keep going back to the cellars. I like it as young and as cool as possible. You wouldn't do it with a Beaujolais Growth or a Bordeaux château wine, but with our wine from the south of Beaujolais, it's not shocking to put ice in the wine. In July and August, I put ice in my glass of Beaujolais."

....

On my first harvest at Château des Granges, I walked through the vineyard with Henri. "Look at those Gamays!" he exclaimed. "The most beautiful of all vines. To make Beaujolais, it has to be Gamay. We're allowed to use up to ten percent maximum of Pinot, Cabernet, or Syrrah, but I don't use them. It would be a whole other experience.

"Yet my soil is more like Burgundy than Beaujolais, and I've always wanted to try and make a vat in the Burgundy style that corresponds to a Burgundy wine. I have the vines, the soil, and the weather. I lack one key factor, the microclimate. My biggest handicap, however, is my workers in the cellar, who are unwilling to treat the wine like a Burgundy. They want the vats of wine, the *cuvées,* to ferment fast like Beaujolais, not left to macerate a long time, as they're thinking about their day off to go hunting!"

We reached a section of the vineyard he had been watching particularly closely. "I've managed to keep this part of the vineyard till the end. Now I must harvest it, take two or three days to finish the wine, and then blend it with my Gamay vats.

"One harvest I managed to make some wine with a good taste of Burgundy; at first, it was hard, tannic, undrinkable. One day in the cellar I heard my cellar master Demoulin offering the wine to his friends to taste. 'I'm going to give you the *cuvée du patron* to taste. Hold on.' Of course the wine shocks them in Beaujolais, and his friends exclaimed, 'What's this invention? It's undrinkable. What's your boss up to?'"

Henri stooped to pick a grape. "These are the Burgundy white grapes. They still need tonight's little rain and tomorrow they'll be firm and superb. It rains at night, and every day the harvesters, tired from work, hope for rain. Yesterday at lunch, when it began to rain, you should have seen them, their eyes shining, thinking: At last, we'll have the day off! But at five minutes to two the rain stopped."

He pointed to a pair of harvesters down one of the rows. "That couple of old Charolais peasants are from my home, from Rambuteau. They come here every year. The one you can't see, picking low down, this is his thirty-second year here. They're very proud and always a hundred yards or so ahead of everyone else, which means sure provocation as there's always another group trying to get ahead and beat them." We watched. "Here comes the little moment of discontent. The pair from Charolais have been beaten, so now pride carries them off on their next row, leaving the young ones far behind."

He indicated another group. "That girl dressed in mauve is Arab. See how gracefully she works, down the rows of vines. All her gestures are graceful. That's her boyfriend with her. Next to them is Debbie from the States, who tells us it's easier to understand the French than the English harvesters. Here comes Adrien with the wheelbarrow to collect their grapes. He's eighty-five, so I wanted to give that job to one of my sons, but he says, No, he's doing fine. The grapes here are small but they make an excellent wine."

· · · · · · · · · ·

The
Winegrower's Story

Pierre, I am a winegrower but
   would that I were not.
At first light, the winegrower
   has to leave his house,
The winds blow, there is work
   to be done.
He carries this tool for cutting,
But the tool does not want
   to cut.
He tries to sharpen it.
It is for pruning the vine.
But still the little devil refuses
   to cut.

—*a Beaujolais winegrower's complaint
inscribed on a late 17th century plate*

"When we bring the harvest in," explained Henri, "we don't press the grapes at first because it spoils them. In Burgundy they press the grapes. Our Gamay needs to go into the vats unspoiled, so we press the grapes after fermentation. We pour out first the juice from the vats, and what's left is pressed. The wine from the vat and the press wine are then mixed. The vat wine is sweet, smooth, and marvelous—we love to drink it just like that, but it needs the tannin from the press wine or it won't keep, it won't age. Some years, though, when the press wine is too bitter and tannic, we only bottle the first wine.

"White wine is produced by pressing the grape at once. Beaujolais is special because it's a red wine made from the Gamay grape's white juice. You can make white wine from Gamay; some Champagne is made from Gamay. Beaujolais obtains its color by fermenting the pulp with the skins. Depending on the year, we leave the wine on the skins, usually about three or four days. One year, in '74, we left them for twelve days. Dreadful, and the yeasts needed warmth to start working.

"It's rare that we obtain from Gamay enough natural alcohol, the twelve or thirteen degrees our clients expect to find in their Beaujolais. We're therefore obliged to add some sugar that some people believe unbalances the wine. In my opinion, sugar that has been properly transformed into alcohol helps bring out the wine's qualities.

"There's a big fight in France. Since Beaujolais is the wine people like to drink in quantity, naturally they would like to have a light Beaujolais without much alcohol. But if you give them that, they don't like it." He shrugged his shoulders and laughed. "On my small estate, I'm not a chemist. I make wine. I taste it. If it's good, I drink it."

Going over to a vat, he took his *tastevin*, the silver tasting cup the wine-grower traditionally carries with him, and drew some wine. He passed it to me.

"Notice that typical taste of leaves. It comes from the grape. Of course, we take care not to let the leaves into the vats. Some wines have it more than others. It can be considered a positive quality.

"In the old days the Beaujolais was bought in the barrel in the cellars. The café owners used to come as soon as the harvest was in and buy their barrels in the cellars. The wine then belonged to them and they'd come to the cellar to care for it, filter it, and fine it. Each village had its professional carters who'd take away the barrels on their carts to Lyon and Saint-Etienne. Saint-Etienne, with its coal miners who worked hard and drank hard, was a region of big Beaujolais drinkers.

"I don't like old Beaujolais. For me, I prefer the Beaujolais of the year. I have a cellar, but there are no old bottles from my estate. We try to make ours fresh and young, whereas the Growths make their wines more as in Burgundy. Some Moulin-à-Vent will last twenty years."

·········

We descended into the underground cellar.

"The wines 'move' here in the cool of the cellar; they continue to live. All the wine moves twice a year—at the time of the blossoming of the vine and again now at harvesttime. It starts to sparkle. I like it sparkling. But you can't bottle it sparkling because the corks would fly out. I like to drink it as early as possible, as cool as possible, from the tap like this.

"These days, we haven't finished harvesting in a good year when the brokers and wine merchants, the *négociants,* are in our cellars tasting and looking for the new wine."

From an average harvest of 1,300,000 hectos of Beaujolais, 450,000 goes as the new wine. Each year, at one minute past midnight on the third Thursday in November, the trucks in the cellars set out into the night to Paris with the first Beaujolais. Today Beaujolais Primeur is called Beaujolais Nouveau, and every Paris bistro hangs out a sign announcing: BEAUJOLAIS NOUVEAU HAS ARRIVED!

The rest of the Beaujolais harvest will be bottled in the spring. Called the Wine of the Year, it will be drunk until the next year's harvest.

"Knowing when to harvest is the difficult decision. Some draw it out so they can harvest very ripe grapes, like going back to the old days. I prefer to harvest when the bouquet is at its fullest, just before complete maturity, so we can retain some acidity and freshness in the wine. In a property like mine, when the whole vineyard is very ripe, it's difficult to bring in all the harvest at once,

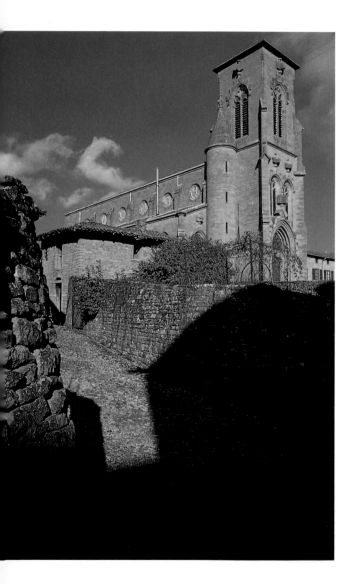

instead of over ten days. Other years, to find what is ripe, I have to move my harvesters around.

"With a big harvest, even with a small harvest, there are those who always make good wines. Others manage to make bad wines even with ripe grapes! Too often it is forgotten that we have to be both winegrower *and* winemaker.

"The Nouveau must be fresh and light and be drunk within a few months. These wines aren't big enough to age, so if they don't sell they remain on our hands. Another problem is stocking our wines. The majority of our Beaujolais has to be sold within the year. Once upon a time the country folk had some reserves; they made wines which could be kept longer, and stored some like bank notes in the cupboard for the bad years. Today everyone, even the rich, needs money every year."

The wine shone in our *tastevins*.

"Beaujolais is the wine that men drink from a water glass. Our water's not good in France. Spoils the stomach. You should drink Beaujolais as new as possible. I start in November when we begin to visit each other. We keep drinking it until next harvesttime, then a short rest to cure our livers, and start again."

. . . .

The harvesters were still at the table so we sat with them. Henri found a new audience. "Beaujolais has the best position on the menus and wine lists in France. Your host in a restaurant wants to please you: he daren't order a carafe wine so he says, 'Give me some Beaujolais.'

"You can drink Beaujolais with anything. It's not a crime to drink Beaujolais with fish. I do and I know others who do. With Beaujolais, the man who knows nothing about wines doesn't have to worry about making a fool of himself. The Frenchman's greatest fear is to make a fool of himself. There are those who know everything, who are pretentious. There are those who don't know and who are intimidated.

"There are no laws." Henri chuckled gleefully. "Drink Beaujolais whenever it gives you pleasure. Of course, you don't drink a bottle of Château Margaux with salad, or a big Burgundy like a Pommard with fish. But there are two French wines which go with every food—Champagne and Beaujolais. I've nothing against a lunch with Champagne throughout. A lunch with Beaujolais makes me feel as if I'm in my home!"

Lunch over, the harvesters left to sit in the sun. Henri remained with me at the table. "Everyone speaks of Beaujolais, everyone drinks it. I once did some research. Traveling a lot at the time by train, going to restaurants in Paris and everywhere, I used to say, 'I'm from Beaujolais.' Immediately everyone began to explain to me how Beaujolais should be made, what it should be like, what it was. I let them talk and then I asked, 'Can you tell me what proportion of wine produced in France is Beaujolais?' Replies varied from eight to thirty percent, some even thought eighty percent, but the average was between twelve and thirteen percent. In fact, the figure is about two percent! Everyone believes Beaujolais is much larger than it is. Legally, the wine you drink with the name Beaujolais can't be anything else but Beaujolais.

"I used to tell my friends, next time you go to Paris, go into a bar with two friends and order some wine: the first one asks for some red wine, the second for a Côtes du Rhône, the third for some Beaujolais. The glasses of wine arrive. 'Red for monsieur, Côtes du Rhône for monsieur, and Beaujolais for monsieur,' says the waiter. Only they'd all come from the same bottle."

At the end of the day, the harvesters returned to the château and Henri addressed his troops. "Okay, you've worked hard. Tomorrow is your day off. Monday, if the weather lets us, we clean up the rest of the rows and move on to the next vineyard. When it's blowing south it brings rain, but sometimes it blows three days before we get rain.

Henri and I returned to the pressing house where they were closing down for the night. Climbing the stairs, I glanced back at the candlelit cellar. It looked like a tiny village square of Beaujolais, deserted after the July Fourteenth festivities. Everyone had left. The place was silent.

....

As the years went by, I came to realize how much Henri enjoyed visitors. Each year he appeared to await my arrival to tell me the next chapter of his Beaujolais story.

One morning we went off in search of the typical "Monsieur Beaujolais." "I

don't think there's a definitive Beaujolais character," he said. "Beaujolais being near Lyon, it's a region of passage with a mixture of people: Gauls, Celts, even families with Saracen roots, as Saracens were invading everywhere in the Middle Ages, riding up rivers like the Romans. The leading traits of a Beaujolais winegrower are his hospitality and sense of humor. In every village, they play farces, tricks, jokes all the time, even on our trips abroad. Nothing very wicked.

"One day last year," Henri recalled over a glass of wine at our first stop, "in a village near here, trying to find someone, I asked a man working in a vineyard if he could direct me. 'Oh,' he said, 'you're a long way away.' We began talking, about the hail and such things. He invited me for a glass of wine, without knowing who I was, and I stayed two hours talking with him in his cellar. That's the Beaujolais."

We passed a vineyard of young vines. "Appellation Beaujolais vines have to be three years old before we can make wine from them. The first year, they have no grapes. The third year, there can be a large crop but it cannot be sold as Beaujolais. Not till the fourth year."

He pointed at a vineyard. "Those are American vines that resist the phylloxera that still exist. I have four or five zinfandel vines in my vineyard. In California, the soil is too good, so rich and the climate so hot, whereas the vine needs to suffer to produce the best grapes. When I took the Beaujolais winegrowers to the Napa Valley, they cried out, 'What fine wines we'd make on those hills.' They saw the vines in valleys of fertile soil where we would put our cattle to graze, grow sugar beets and vegetables. In Australia, we were astounded to see how high they grow their vines. 'We have to because of the harvesting machines,' we were told. I said nothing. And of course it's strange to see them pruning the vines in August. In a restaurant in Sydney, the owner brought out a bottle of his favorite Beaujolais, a Primeur five years old! 'That's too old for a Primeur,' I told him. 'Oh, no, sir,' he said, 'Primeur means the best.' In Australia we found that some wineries had been trying to sell what they called Beaujolais, made in Australia, and announcing, 'Beware of the French copies!'

"The Côtes du Rhône, excellent wines, have tried to go after the Nouveau market that we launched. Naturally we're delighted that our colleagues are treading the same path we laid. But as Parisians say, since when did Madame Chantal in her salon in the Faubourg offer her services at the same price as the ladies you see standing in the Rue Saint-Denis?"

We passed the largest château in Beaujolais, Château de la Chaize. "In the seventeenth century, Madame de Sévigné visited La Chaize and sent word home: 'I am writing you from this little Beaujolais village.' The Roussy de Sales who own this fine château are old family friends."

Then we were in Le Breuil, where Henri appeared to know everyone. "There's the prettiest lady in Le Breuil going to confession. Never run over the pretty ones!" A man crossed the road carrying a fishing line. "He's caught some trout. Once our commune's chief engineer, today he's one of the happy retired ones living at the expense of society. He does a little fishing, though his fishing net is far from legal.

"That young man going into the bistro carries the coffins at funerals. Here it's the young who do that work, unpaid, though they're given a light lunch. After the burial, they go off to the café and, at the expense of the dead man's family, eat and drink deeply, which restores morale to the rest of the community."

At the bistro, a new young mayor needed to see Henri. "Like all new mayors he's going to do miracles," said Henri afterward. "Our electric lines were built by the syndicate I'm president of, and this nice gentleman does the work for us. Naturally, he does everything as costly as possible because that means the best work. Our syndicate of twenty-five communes pay dues, and some of the mayors request enormous work since it's not they who pay but the neighbors. I have to be sure there's some justice, so meeting him today, I've done a good day's work."

In the bakery in the center of the neighboring village, Bois d'Oignt, Henri bought bread. "*Bonjour, madame.* Your young lady is so charming," he told the baker's wife. "I'm in love with her smile. One comes here for her smile. So pretty, always smiling and gracious, since she got married last month."

"*Monsieur le comte* knows everything," said the baker's wife, warm and homely like her bread.

"Life is serious, *madame,* but sometimes we like to joke."

The church bell of Bois d'Oignt struck noon. Walking across the square to the grocery, Henri greeted an old lady in black coming out of the store. "Why, here comes the prettiest lady of Bois d'Oignt." He gave her a big smile. "See, she has the prettiest eyes in Bois d'Oignt."

The lady smiled back good-humoredly. Everyone was used to Henri's sense of fun. As we entered the bar of the Hôtel de France on the square, the locals greeted us. *"Bonjour, monsieur le maire."*

Henri introduced me. "*Bonjour, messieurs,* meet an old friend, an English-man living in America. He was my guide on my first trips to America for

Beaujolais and we became good friends. He's nice to have around and returns here often, like a child of Beaujolais. He speaks French well, and is starting to speak Beaujolais."

Henri laughed and ordered *canons* of Beaujolais for everyone.

"You see," he explained to me, "we meet in cafés, we go to each other's homes in Beaujolais. We still maintain that conviviality of the village."

"Where there are no more cafés, life is dead," said one of the men. "Life in a village is the café."

"The church, the school, and the café," Henri added.

Glasses were refilled.

"As soon as the harvest is ready to be tasted in early November," Henri was saying, "you cannot go through a village without everyone you know greeting you, 'Here, come and taste what I've made.' You go down into the cellar. A neighbor arrives. We all go and taste at the neighbor's. Finally they come back to your place. By evening you're pretty tired. When you're in a neighbor's cellar," he confides, "*never* say that a wine is bad. One drinks it. One says, 'Ah.' One offers no criticism. One says it's good. And one drinks full glasses."

....

Henri looked at his watch. "We're just in time for lunch. One talks in Beaujolais about the Beaujolais quarter of an hour. It means at least fifteen minutes late. It makes me furious. I say, why fix a meeting at eleven o'clock if they arrive at eleven thirty? It's impossible."

Driving up to Henri's château, we passed the kitchen garden. "We never buy vegetables. Much cheaper to produce them, and they taste so much better. You should see our potatoes, what beauties, though the best are those of my workers. I give them a little land and they grow the best potatoes."

We could smell the flowering of the vine. "A very soft smell," said Henri. "Each grape variety has its own smell. When all the flowers come out at the same time, it smells even stronger, very honey. Fine weather at flowering time is a good sign for the harvest. The maturity afterward is guaranteed."

He stood looking at his home. "I was born in the Charolais some miles north of here, but Les Granges has been my home for thirty or forty years."

He saw his son on the way down the hill for the midday meal. "A good lad, Claude has character and a generous heart. He's tough, too."

We all went in for lunch. Irline's *foie gras* reminded me of Alain Querre in Saint-Emilion who bought his fresh livers at the markets in the Landes region.

"That's the expensive way," said Henri. "Here, we raise the geese and we eat them. For three weeks Irline is a slave. She cannot go out, force-feeding the geese morning and evening. You hold them by the neck and force the maize down a funnel. The maize must be a year old, so it's still expensive and a lot of work."

Henri poured a bottle of Beaujolais from his cellar. "It's last year's wine. Not a great big wine like a Burgundy, but a happy, very pretty wine that I drink until the next harvest. After that it doesn't interest me anymore. In my cellar, I've some bottles of Bordeaux and Burgundy, and if I have Beaujolais in bottle, it's Moulin-à-Vent. When I need some wine, I go down to the barrel. The wine keeps a little of its carbonic gas. Before, Beaujolais never traveled. Now it travels perfectly. That's technical progress for you!

"There are certainly advantages, not only administrative, in the wine going to the *négociant*. Today, in France or abroad, the customer does not accept the least sign of sediment in a bottle. As a child I remember when my parents had the glasses out after a meal, we children would steal into the dining room to finish what remained in the glasses, often some very good wine and full of

sediment. I'm shocked to see these very old bottles of Burgundy with no sediment. But customers won't take the wine unless it's been filtered, often too filtered. There's yet one more technical operation: the new wines that keep a little of their carbonic gas are now decarbonized. Again, we call that technical progress."

··········

One evening, Henri and I were sitting after dinner in the drawing room of the eighteenth-century château. The heavy curtains of embroidered pink damask, vestiges of Henri's days in the Lyon silk business, hung like bands of color against the gray and gold room. A log fire was smoldering in the hearth. Henri spoke in a deep, quiet voice like a man who had walked far and now took his time to pause and think aloud. Irline, away from her kitchen, sat listening, beautiful by the light of the fire. In the other room sat their children, young men now, their eyes still riveted on television.

Henri talked into the fire. "We are like people in the last century who built the hackney carriages, the most beautiful carriages in the world, but then they were 'out,' replaced by the automobile. The world goes faster and faster. Many countries envy and dream of our tranquil life and traditions. An evening like this by the fire is no longer possible in modern civilization.

"It's ridiculous, the two of us, Irline and I, living in this immense château built for five servants. We live here, limping along. When I have a little money to invest, I say to Irline we'll repaint the staircase, replace the carpeting, install heating, we'll make this house better. But is it worthwhile? I'm sixty-two years old. In fifteen years I shall not be here, normally. She will last ten years longer; she's much younger and much less used."

Irline laughed gently to herself.

"These investments for twenty years, are they worth it? I don't see any of my children living here."

Silence. The fire crackled in the hearth. Henri sounded unusually resigned and mellow. We sipped a liqueur, a marc d'Auvergne.

"During the war, I knew an old farmer who had only a coat, no shoes. He wore clogs. He was a very religious man—got up early, milked his cows, then walked to the village to Mass and to collect his bread. He returned home and

Two Ways to Cook a Sausage

During harvesttime at Château des Granges, Irline de Rambuteau prepares her Lyon-style sausage, *cervelas* (highly seasoned smoked pork sausage). She places her sausage in a *cocotte*, or earthenware pot, covers it with some liqueur (*marc d'Auvergne* or fresh *marc* from the wine press), and leaves it to cook for four or five minutes. She adds half a bottle of young Beaujolais, closes the lid tightly, and allows it to simmer. Half an hour later, she pours in the rest of the wine and brings it to a boil. Reducing the juice to a sauce, she cuts the sausage into slices and serves with boiled potatoes or rice, with a Beaujolais.

The winegrower in the vineyard has his own version. He wraps the sausages in tubes of aluminum foil, twisted tightly at one end. He then pours in the Beaujolais, saturating the pierced sausages, twists the open end tightly, and places the sausages on the grill or embers of his fire. He turns them over several times so that they are cooked through. Carefully removing the foil and allowing them to cool a moment, he cuts the sausages into slices with his sharp opel knife and serves them with country bread and his Beaujolais.

worked his fields with two cows who didn't move fast. What he did in three days, my son Claude does in one hour with my tractor. This man was happy. He was a thinker. He didn't have the radio or newspapers. They told him the news when he went to the village. But he reasoned much better than people do today. Some might say he was a slave. Not true.

"The country folk I knew as a child worked ten or fifteen hours a day. They worked slowly. They lost a whole day going to the barber. The city worker does eight hours five days a week, has two hours of subway, and paperwork to do when he gets home.

"The old peasant had his leisure *naturally*. He worked his fields with his plow, and the moment he finished, his free time began. Today you work for what? Vacations: jumping into a car, fighting one's way down autoroutes, packed into a camping site where one's condemned to live even more restricted than at home.

"Adrien works for me, sits at our table at mealtimes, and is a free man. Every morning he has his habits. He cuts some wood. Today it was raining, so he cuts a little more, to stay out of the rain."

The fire had become a bed of embers, the marc glowed at the bottom of my glass. It was time for bed. The sons had left the television and were in their rooms under the roof. My bedroom was the splendid one with a period canopy four-poster bed in which, Irline said, she and Henri had slept when they were first married. The striped roses on the wallpaper matched the curtains. Bed, curtains, and wallpaper must have been of the same period as this part of the château, late eighteenth century. The warmth of goose feathers of the bed cover restored a sense of well-being.

It was the last time I was to see Henri. Early spring when I called from America to announce I was working on the final draft of this book, Henri told me, "Come over, I will tell you the rest of the Beaujolais story." I did not know that cancer was taking over, and a few weeks later, after returning from his son's wedding in the Périgord, Henri was gone.

His lifelong friend Gerard Canard succeeded him as president of the Compagnons du Beaujolais. Over many more *canons* of Beaujolais at the Annexe and out in the cellars of the villages, in true Beaujolais style, Gerard introduced me to more winegrowers and *négociants*. "I promised Henri in the hospital that I would do all I can for you, in his place."

THE WINEGROWER'S STORY

When I traveled around Beaujolais with Henri, our points of departure and return had always been his château. Out on the wine road alone, I found myself man to man with the winegrowers, sitting in their cellars, cafés, and homes, their privileged guest as I listened.

Louis Brechard, at eighty-four affectionately called "Papa" Brechard, once deputy for Beaujolais in the French National Assembly, was a past president of the Union Interprofessionnelle and one of the leaders in organizing the first cooperatives. Nicknamed "The Lion of the Valley," he has always been a "battler, a man of action and vigor, national and regional action and vigor, a leader of rare intelligence and understanding," as one *négociant* described him.

Papa Brechard invited me to the village of Chenelette where he was born. The *pot* of Beaujolais on the table, we sat in the last of the cafés. A decade back, Chenelette boasted five busy cafés. "I was eleven years old and my father never came back from the 14–18 War. There was no one. No more teachers, no more priests, nobody anywhere. Everyone had left."

During the last century his great-grandparents had been artisans with a cloth store in Lyon and a hectare of vines in Chenelette. Business grew bad in the 1850s and the vineyards were attacked by mildew and phylloxera. Aged

twelve and with a good memory, Brechard passed his school exams, winning a coveted departmental prize. "Next morning I was out working in the vineyard. No pay." He laughed. "They gave us five francs on Sunday. They couldn't do better. But we had to eat, to dress a little."

All the work was manual. "Before phylloxera, you laid the vine down, it took root and grew up again a little further on—one vine here, another over there, another beyond that. This way the vine was eternal, or nearly. A vine after four years of life was finished. Today, phylloxera will eat the roots if they go deep down, so we're obliged to renew our vines by grafting them with American stock."

Winemaking was a folk tradition. "Some remarkable wines were made: remarkable years and remarkable winemakers. There were also the others, many others. Men of the soil, we made our wines using what they call in Bordeaux *le pifometre,* the nose. We lodged our wine in wood. No one called the new wine Primeur or New Beaujolais then. We country folk called it *vin bourru.* The mousse on top of the fermenting vat was the *bourre.*"

Brechard recalled Lyon and its bistros. "Their owners knew their wines and would be out here in the vineyards before harvesting began, choosing their part of the harvest. They'd bring their empty 215-liter barrels with them by rail and stand near the vats watching the fermentation. We'd make holes in the vat and stick in two or three straws for the gases to escape. At fermentation time, they'd draw off their wine directly into barrels, plugging them loosely so the wine would not burst out. The barrels were carted off to town by horse or oxen. When temperatures were normal, we had some absolutely remarkable wines. At other times, we were left with vinegar.

"Besides Lyon, our big market was nearby Saint-Etienne where the miners took our fermenting wines with their lunch boxes down into the mines. Miners were big drinkers. Understandably, as it's a terrible profession. While deputy for the Beaujolais region, in 1972 I spent a half day down a mine, and promised myself, never again.

"The 28,000 hectares of Beaujolais stretched everywhere, until 1952 when we drew the boundaries correctly, severely reducing Beaujolais to 12,000 hectares. Today we're back up to 22,500."

Papa Brechard is the proud father of the cooperative cellars in Beaujolais, the oldest of which dates from 1928. The first cooperatives shocked everyone, but all Beaujolais benefited from them. They brought in technological improvements for small winegrowers who lacked the means to install modern equipment, and the quality of wines improved throughout the Beaujolais.

The winegrower could bring his grapes into the cooperative that then made the wine and relieved him of many worries. "We tried to maintain the winegrower's presence within the cooperative through meetings, tastings, participation in management. That way the cooperative played its role more fully."

The View from the Windmill

ROMANÈCHE (Saône-et-Loire) - Moulin à Vent
Vins renommés

FROM AN UPSTAIRS window of the windmill at Moulin-à-Vent, the geologist Pierre Combier explained how he views the vineyards. "Beaujolais is between two areas: *Le Nord* (northern France), and *Le Midi* (the area bordering the Mediterranean). Some say the boundary is farther down the Rhône Valley at Pont d'Isere, on the 49th Parallel, where there's a monument depicting a woman of the Nord meeting a woman of the Midi. Our micro-climate recalls the Midi. You can see the boundary clearly here. Look at our roofs with hollow tiles of Roman origin, rounded and placed together like boot tops. Look further north to Alsace; the roofs are more pointed, built against rain and snow.

"Our region lies east of the Massif Central plateau, on the extreme edge of the Jura mountains and the Alps, with the great plain of Les Dombes below. The rivers descend from the mountains: the Sâone from the Juras, and the Rhône from the Alps. They meet at Lyon, bringing down with them the snows of winter into the Mediterranean.

"During the Ice Age, a vast field of moving glaciers stretched from the Alps. Advancing as far as Lyon, they deposited immense rocks that formed the hills around the city. The soil of Les Dombes plain was derived from these glaciers, and today is full of lakes and ponds, perched over an

impermeable subsoil. Beaujolais was formed by soils deposited through the Primary, Secondary, and Tertiary Ages. Our granite is from the Primary Age."

Pierre Combier believes soil influences the wine much more than people realize. "At harvesttime in my vineyard, I amuse myself by following a small, rich seam of manganese that goes obliquely across the vineyard. Moulin-à-Vent and Chenas are built on similar seams, producing a characteristic taste from the soil. The decomposed granite is ideal soil for our Gamay.

"The color of our stone houses comes from particles in the granite—crystals of minerals like quartz, mica, and orthoclase—that weather and decompose into clay. The crystals, one on top of the other in the granite, give this rock its blond color."

Beaujolais was once considered part of the map of Burgundy and for some, it still is. Others, enthused by the unparalleled success and popularity of the wine, believe Beaujolais belongs to Beaujolais. "The Burgundians achieved their reputation long before we did," said Brechard. "A great reputation, which may have led to a certain sense of nobility that some call superiority. Despite a certain condescension for our Beaujolais *négociants,* they continue to come and buy our wines.

"The big wine houses of Burgundy like the Latours, Jadot, and company had good reason to be proud. Burgundy makes wines primarily to keep, the *vins de garde,*" said Brechard. "We make wines, first of all the Beaujolais Nouveau, to be drunk within the year. Even our Grands Crus—Moulin-à-Vent, Fleurie, and Juliénas—are for drinking within four or five years in a good vintage."

Brechard has been a staunch defender of the *appellations,* the laws that allow the Beaujolais Crus to be labeled also Appellation Bourgogne, a practice largely ceased by Burgundy wine merchants today who prefer to sell them as Moulin-à-Vent, Fleurie, or Juliénas. "A remarkable creation, *appellation d'origine.* It forces wine regions to be responsible for their own *appellations.* Before these laws, people made wine and called it Beaujolais or whatever name they pleased."

Brechard's advice to young winegrowers was as father to son. "In our time we've made errors, but I say quality, quality, quality, and possibly even more severe controls. I can talk like this at my age. I'm not looking for popularity. If you want to make good Beaujolais, avoid the mechanical harvester at all costs. It's not allowed here and must continue to be banned. Beaujolais's future depends on more discipline, on improving technique and the presentation of our wines. First, subordinate everything to improving quality. Perhaps it means we produce half as much, but we'll make better-quality wine. You can never make a wine of quality at ten francs the bottle. Impossible."

He greatly admired Henri de Rambuteau. "He had style, charisma, passion, an astonishing awareness of life. An extraordinary being. One day a car came speeding through my village, made a U-turn, and pulled up alongside me. It was Rambuteau. Getting out of his car, he greeted me, 'I've a good story for you.' Unable to restrain myself, I said, 'You did that just to tell me a story, you bloody fool!' We went into the café for a glass of wine. Men of such ability and vigor are irreplaceable."

Brechard took my hand and said, "I have a little time left and, thanks to Beaujolais, I can say that life around here has not been so disagreeable."

··········

Over the hill in another valley, at Saint-Laurent-d'Oignt, was Johannes Papillon, a winegrower of the same generation as Brechard but dwelling much closer to the soil. Papillon now lived in retirement with his wife in a small house made of *pierres dorées,* a local stone with a golden color. We sat in the kitchen, a bottle of his Beaujolais and four glasses on the oilcloth-covered table. The door was open to the vineyards that went up to the top two inches of sky. The cat sat at the door watching the courtyard. Nothing stirred.

"For us," said Madame Papillon, "it's a little lost here. I grew up till I was eighteen in Lyon. I still miss my Lyon. Life's difficult in Beaujolais, difficult to make a living."

"Difficult everywhere," said Papillon. He wore a bright blue wool jacket and an old aqua T-shirt open at the neck, a wonderful mix of colors in this quiet house. "We didn't build the house. I'm the third generation, my grandfather was born here and is dead, my father born here and dead, and I have spent all my life here and will shortly be gone. With my son, that's four generations in the same house.

"I learned young that my parents were living in misery," he recalled. "Wine wasn't selling. When I began, I worked for nothing; my parents never thought of paying us. No vacations. I married my wife to get a wage." Madame Papillon feigned surprise. "We still work Saturdays and Sundays. We had cows and corn, but they don't go well with vines. The vine is a full-time occupation. But when a harvest could be lost, you had to have something else to bring in a living.

"I began with one horse to bring in the grapes. No mechanical harvester will ever get up and down these hillsides. We'd throw the harvest into the vats, and since we knew nothing about winemaking, the wine made itself. We watched it begin to bubble, and the froth, all rosy, spread up over the vat. When the vat

dropped down, we'd work through the night drawing off the wine, to make room for the next day's harvest. Harvesting went better then, perhaps. We could find competent workers, often from Lyon. We had a small team of workers; when the parents grew too old, the children took their place. Today it's hard to get them to work eight hours. They only come to meet a girl. At harvest festival in our house, the last evening together, we sang, the harvest menu was a little more ample, and we drank several good bottles."

Johannes Papillon, alongside Papa Brechard, was one of the pioneers in the cooperative movement in his little village, Saint-Laurent. "Our cooperative is me," declared Papillon with pride. "I was thirty years in its service, till my retirement in 1990. With Père Brechard, we were five winegrowers who built it. We were criticized, ostracized, made scapegoats at first. Old traditions die hard. But someone had to dare to do it.

"I can see my father visiting a friend to taste the new wines in his cellar. How they liked to keep their wines in their cellars! The arrival of the cooperative meant the cellar was bare, nothing there. When you brought your grapes to the cooperative, if you wanted some bottles of your wine, you had to go over to the cooperative for them. Cellar days were over.

"Our cooperatives made wines of quality. No more grapes in ancient wooden vats, no more winemaking any which way. But it took time to convince the winegrowers. We employed an oenologist, a serious young man from the village whom we sent off to Beaune to learn the technique of winemaking. Altogether, it was a new and good departure for the Beaujolais vineyard. It was at a time when the young men were leaving for the town. We had to do something.

"We'd built a cooperative for 10,000 hectos of wine, but the first harvest brought us in barely 4,500 hectos, but of high quality. The ones who liked working together saw its potential. The older ones stood aside, and the young ones became the leaders. The word was out: the quality of the new wine at the cooperative was good.

"Then came the selling of the wine. We needed money. We found a wine merchant and told him, 'We've ten cases to sell.' He gave us his price. It was so low, we knew this was not how a good cooperative should be run.

"One day Monsieur Georges Duboeuf, the *négociant,* came to our cellar to buy two or three vats of wine. That went on for four or five years. He would say,

ROMANÈCHE-THORINS — Mines de Manganèse
Les mines de manganèse exploitées depuis 1829 occupent environ 50 ouvriers et produisent par an 2.090 tonnes de minerai

'That vat pleases me. I'll take it all.' We began to understand each other. He said, 'If you like, we can make a contract.' Ever since, it has been marvelous. We never lose one centime. He buys all our wine, advises us on winemaking and selling, and sometimes criticizes us, gently, without making a big thing of it. I'd go over to Romanèche and discuss things with him, ask him how he saw the year ahead. I'd see him after harvest with a hundred bottles on the table, samples from vats for him to taste and analyze. Every two months I went to his office for the payment on account, took it to our bank, and we distributed it

among the members of the cooperative. Never had to wait for it, not like others elsewhere less fortunate. When I needed to phone him, six in the morning was the best time for him. He was there and always glad to see me.

"But you couldn't start a cooperative today without those leaders who've sacrificed so much to give Beaujolais its rightful place. It's more difficult for the young to succeed us. They haven't known the hard years we've gone through, when morale was at zero. They bring their wines to the cooperative and stand there waiting for their checks. I worry that future generations may not understand that the price they ask should be correct. If they go overboard, it can ruin everything."

....

The Fête des Crus at Chiroubles in April gathers winegrowers from all over Beaujolais. On the square, the trumpets of the village brass band heralded this year's winners of the best wines tasted early in the morning by an international panel of bleary-eyed judges. In the green and white striped official tent, the Compagnons du Beaujolais honored the memory of the turn-of-the-century industrialist inventor Victor Vermorel, born in Beaujolais's capital, Villefranche. His 1910 work on grape varieties of the world, *L'Ampélographie*—seven volumes of 800 engravings, 1,200 pages in all—had been reedited and published by Madame Jeanne Laffitte of Marseille.

The other guest of honor was also from the Midi. Denis Boulbas, professor of viticulture at Montpellier University and publisher of *La Revue Viticole,* fervently addressed the assembled winegrowers.

"Mesdames, messieurs, my friends, winegrowers of Beaujolais, your grape the black Gamay with white juice you will find in Vermorel's fine book—surely the heaviest book in France. Victor Vermorel knew how to place science at the service of our vineyards. In 1883 he assembled a team of eighty-five collaborators in fourteen different countries in an age with neither telephone nor fax. A remarkable feat of perseverance under a difficult economy not unlike ours today. Vermorel was the inventor of the vineyard spray. People would say, 'I'll go spray the vines with my Vermorel.'

"This Gamay you are so fortunate to possess almost exclusively. Out of a total of 30,000 hectares of Gamay in the world, you have 22,500 hectares. When I walk in certain vineyards around the world and feel under my feet some granite soil, I say to myself, 'What excellent Gamay one could grow here.' But I keep that to myself. I say *nothing!* One day I was in Shenyang, the Saint-Tropez of China. A remarkable place where one could grow the Gamay and even wines to age. But I told them *nothing!*

"Use the Gamay," he continued. "You will have good wine. Your only competition are the winegrowers of California, who've never understood the Gamay with their Napa Gamay, an ordinary grape variety originating from our Massif Central. The Australian Gamay that was troubling you when they tried to call it Beaujolais is not a true Gamay. You are the world masters of production and sales of Gamay.

"In these difficult times—difficult, I'm told, even for Beaujolais Crus—do not despair! We are going, mesdames and messieurs, toward a Europe that will be cloudy with few luminous points ahead, a Europe where everything may fall apart and France may no longer exist. But I tell you, Beaujolais will be there! Beaujolais will be one of those luminous lights, shining through for us."

....

Jean Dutraive, president of the winegrowers' union that represents the interests of the 4,800 vineyards of Beaujolais, is a substantial, expressive man. He greeted me at his château in Fleurie with a big warm smile and handshake. Dutraive knows his typical Beaujolais winegrower. "He's very open, naturally hospitable, believes in his profession, is very attached to his soil. He can be slow to accept change. His family has always been here and intends to remain. The younger generation, however, shows considerable evolution. They have technical training that opens doors. They have visited other wine regions to see what is going on. This looks well for the future of the region."

Beaujolais, for Jean Dutraive, is still part of the map of Burgundy. The annual production of Beaujolais amounts to more than half the annual volume of Burgundy wines. Beaujolais was first known by its Moulin-à-Vent, still listed among the Burgundies by some Burgundy shippers.

"The Interprofession and our union group two Beaujolais families: the winegrowers family and the wine merchants family. One of our main roles has been to uphold the *appellations* which, back in the thirties, the wine merchants didn't see much need of. Today our *appellations* belong to us, with laws laid down by the French government office, L'Institut National des Appellations d'Origine, INAO, working in direct consultation with us winegrowers and the wine merchants. We have to defend our profession, our *appellations,* and our land."

Beaujolais could hardly find a more solid defender. "One of our biggest dangers is the autoroute. The Lyon-Bordeaux autoroute was originally drawn to pass just south of our vineyards, right in front of Henri de Rambuteau's château. Then came another plan that avoided the vineyards. Then everything was scrapped and a new plan ran the autoroute further north, right through the vineyards. The winegrower has nowhere else to go. All we ask is that they avoid the vineyards that are a treasure of France. It's as if they put an autoroute through the Place de la Concorde in Paris. But to big technocrats, we're a long way away from their office when they make their plans."

Dutraive's vineyard is in Fleurie, but, as is often the case in Beaujolais, he shares family property in other Crus. "My first year, the rain flooded our harvesting. It had hailed earlier in the year and thirty to forty percent of the crop was destroyed; my second year, ninety percent was destroyed. The hail passes, often in a matter of ten minutes, piercing everything in its path with hail as fine as grain or big as billiard balls. Generally it arrives with a big wind coming down from the mountains, and follows the corridor of a valley. The worst are the ones that return—you see a storm going away, think it's over. Suddenly the wind changes, it's back, a strange-colored cloud you know is hail. Where will it land? It can attack one village or several villages along a belt five or six kilometers long. Because of the mountains, it is often followed by a heavy storm.

"We never see frost here, but the vines in Chiroubles at four hundred meters altitude get frost. Drought is something else. We see the vine suffering but we're not allowed to water them. If the leaves dry up and fall off, the vine never recovers that year. If the leaves manage to survive a drought, the vine recovers.

"Our land is granitic and the rock is always just below the thin soil. The wine's character comes from this rocky subsoil. Over in Brouilly their wines differ from Côte de Brouilly wines from the mountain with its extremely tough blue granite stone. And the wines from the south side of the mountain differ from those from the north."

We tasted some Fleurie that he had aged. "You have to taste wines often to recognize them. Taste a Fleurie from near Moulin-à-Vent, you could mistake it for a Moulin-à-Vent. Or a Fleurie from near Chiroubles, you might hesitate between calling it one or the other. When you're right in the heart of Fleurie, you find the character."

Jean Dutraive disapproves of blind adherence to vintage reports. "When the press talks about a harvest and gives it a rating, some consumers who don't know so much about wines drink with that rating in their head. If the vintage rating is low, they don't buy a wine." Turning the wine around in the glass, he smelled it. "These in this vat are from my old vines, so for the aromas in the

wine to come out, you have to oxygenate it well. See them coming out now! Since last year we're using yeasts that are partly from Gamay. Our yeasts used to come from Côtes du Rhône and other regions, like that 71B yeast some say gives a taste of bananas. Now we have a local one. At harvesttime, natural yeasts, good and bad, are in the grapes, in the vats, all over."

Jean Dutraive's son works with his father in the business. "What's extraordinary today is that our sons are going to wine school to learn the technique of winemaking. When they take over the family property, they want to exercise their profession fully and make their own wine. I quite see that the cooperative is the answer for small vineyards without the means to modernize or to buy stainless steel vats, so they benefit from a collective's equipment. Fine. But if you have ten or even seven or eight hectares, make your own wine. Otherwise, you're abandoning your profession!"

The plate of *charcuterie* on the barrel was from his butcher in Fleurie. "He comes to the house each year to kill the pig. We make the sausage and hang it in a little cellar so that it gathers mold. Ham, too, has to be salted for one or two months depending on its size. It needs air not too dry and humidity not too humid, so we hang it in a cellar. We could make excellent sausages here in the wine cellar, but it wouldn't last long, with the visitors."

· · · · · · · · · ·

Up the road from Fleurie is Moulin-à-Vent and its old windmill that gave its name to the village. Inside the windmill, wooden stairs lead to a loft and a view over the vineyards and the Saône Valley below.

"Downstairs they delivered and sorted the various qualities of corn," explained André Sauguet proudly. His family has owned the mill since 1749. "There are two stones, one fixed to the floor, the other in the milling mechanism that runs off the wings in the wind. The roof was so light it could turn to face the wind. We get three winds: the cold north wind, the warm and humid southerly or Mediterranean wind, and the westerly crosswind, *la traversée,* from the Atlantic Ocean. Our microclimate is continental, also influenced by the Mediterranean and Atlantic. Like all great vineyard regions, we have a reserve of water nearby; just as Bordeaux has rivers that balance the temperature, we have the Saône in the valley below."

When life was difficult in Beaujolais, the tradesmen in a village played the role of banker. "The baker kept a notebook for each client and jotted down the daily quantity of bread taken. At the end of the month, or more often at the end of the year or when the wine was sold, we went to pay the baker. Nearly all the tradesmen did likewise, including the blacksmith, and sometimes the butcher, though one ate meat less often than today. The baker also bought his flour on credit from the miller. The miller paid for the corn in installments. We lived in a closed circle—shops, cafés, and at the heart of the village, the church and the mayor's office. The only place where there was no credit was at the café.

"Every village or hamlet had an oven where they made the bread. A blackboard listed the day and hour allotted to each inhabitant to bake his bread for the week."

I remembered Christmas in Paris when we took the turkey around to the baker to be roasted after he had finished baking the day's bread.

"Friends of the baker still do that here," said André Sauguet.

....

CLOS DU MOULIN-A-VENT
(Marque déposée)
Monopole de Jean DESMARQUEST
P^{re} au MOULIN-A-VENT (S.-et-L.)

Le Vignoble

Les Vendanges

Le Pressurage

In the Moulin-à-Vent tasting room, a group of winegrowers were seated around a long dark oak table with glasses of Beaujolais, waiting to meet me. No one escapes visiting the cellar. "In Beaujolais, it's fatal," said André with a laugh. "There's no way out; one finishes by going into the cellar to taste the wine. When working outdoors, we often go on a tour of the cellars. We don't wait for it to rain."

"Moulin-à-Vent and Beaujolais were the two popular wines largely consumed in the cafés of Lyon," explained one of the winegrowers. "The drivers took a day to descend the fifty kilometers of road to Lyon. At the top of the hill into the city, there was a café that hired out a fresh horse. The horse knew its own way home. The café owners reserved their two or three barrels a year for their clientele, bottling the wine themselves and serving it in the *pot*. You ordered a *pot* of Beaujolais, not a glass. The players at a game of bowls lined up one meter of *pots,* thirteen of them. A *pot* containing forty-five centiliters of wine was a bottle with a thick, heavy glass base that gave it stability. It didn't

fall over or break easily. Even the glasses had thick bases. You don't see many *pots* about these days."

"You frequented a bistro because his wine was good," added another.

"My grandfather was a barrelmaker," said the oldest of the winegrowers. "The container used to cost more than the wine. The wine was shipped for a price that included wine and barrel. They were not the oak barrels we know, but were made of chestnut. Every commune had its barrelmaker. Today we're the only commune with a sizable manufacturer of barrels, who ships the world over."

One of the winegrowers announced a new moon tonight. "We still take the moon into account for certain work. We prune young vines at new moon in March when the vegetation is thicker. We say, 'Prune early, prune late, prune best in March.'" Pruning leaves a wound on the vine. December pruning means the vegetation is sparse, with the wound open a month without healing, prey to diseases. March pruning means the wound heals fast.

"The pruning finished," said another, "the children come around after school to pick up the vine cuttings and bring them home to heat the oven for the bread baking. Here everything has its use. The wood of the vine provides energy to heat the ovens for the baker and to heat the water for the weekly washing. We cut the *vîmes* that tie the vines, at home in groups during the *veillée,* the evening family gathering. There was a time when the *veillée* took place in the stable, where it was warm because of the animals, the cows providing the central heating as we sat around on stools by the light of an oil lamp."

The valley of the Saône and the Dombes plain lay below us. "We go there to hunt game in the marshes, to fish the carp in the lakes. It is where we find the much-prized hens of Bresse. But our everyday food, like the wine, comes from around here. It was always soup for dinner in the evening, and whatever was left over we ate next morning before going out to prune the vines. We killed the pig, and from the farmyard we had hens, eggs, rabbits, milk. That was how we lived and survived during the 39–45 War. In difficult times, one is terribly concerned with the problems of everyday survival: getting up early and working late, adapting as best we could, the day's schedule according to the weather. Night didn't always mean we stopped work. We prepared for the next season after dark, by the light of the fire: cutting pickets, preparing the *vîmes.* We got up before it was light and worked well after sunset, into the night. For country folk, life depends on the weather."

··········

Château de la Chaize is the grandest *domaine* in the Beaujolais. Jules Mansart, architect of the Palace of Versailles for Louis XIV, signed the plans of the château. The gardens are by André Le Nôtre, who also designed the park at Versailles and, in Paris, the gardens of the Tuileries and the great sweep up the avenue of the Champs-Élysees from the Louvre.

A damp gray early-morning mist hung over La Chaize. The iron gates were locked. As I walked up the drive, my shoes on the stones echoed across the deserted park. I lifted the heavy iron knocker on the oak door and knocked. Silence. I knocked again. Nicole, Marquise Roussy de Sales, welcomed me into the living room with its wide fireplace. On the wall hung a haunting painting of the château in the days of the Sun King.

"La Chaize has never left our family," she explained, "I've been running the château over twenty years, having succeeded my great-aunt Madame de Montague who died at the age of ninety-six. Henri de Rambuteau knew her extremely well." She laughed. "Their relationship was a total extravagance!

"You should see the château on a fine day, with its exceptional site up against the hillside with the vineyards behind, and the woods above and fields forming a half-circle. I've never understood why this château wasn't demolished in the Revolution, or didn't suffer during the Occupations. Even in the last war they were content just to take the wines."

I asked about her Beaujolais winegrowers. "We have families who've been here for generations. Two sons are about to take over from their father; the grandfather was there before them. They still talk of 'grandfather's land.' Because they work on sections of vineyard here and there, from time to time I try to reorganize them. But always I hear the same story: 'This is my great-grandfather's vineyard, he cultivated it, I don't wish to change it for another elsewhere.' Attached as they are to their land, sometimes I'm obliged to say, 'Now, that's the past . . .' The old contracts with the *métayers* are strict, and most favorable toward them. Their sons have the right to take their place when they retire, unless there are real problems. The same laws as in Bordeaux prevent me from working the land entirely myself."

The winegrowers accepted a woman in charge at the château. "Before me they got used to my great-aunt, an extraordinary character. The men in the Montague family were often soldiers, often away. The women ran the place—sold the wine, settled disputes, asked that bills be paid. There are several beautiful properties around here that belong to women. If we were no good, the château wouldn't work. I am here because my great-aunt decided that it should be me in the family who was installed here with my husband, who, until his death, was export director at Christian Dior. She knew he was good for the château image and, like all women, found him most attractive. She saw me as

capable of looking after the house and vineyards. She lived here from June to November, the rest of the year in Paris exchanging letters with her manager, her *régisseur.* Those days and ways, she realized, were over.

"My husband and I were advised to bring the wine into the château: make it, bottle it on the property, and market it ourselves. I can afford the luxury of assembling vines of different ages, from different exposures of the vineyard, giving me a wine of character and authenticity. Depending on the year, our ninety-seven hectares of vines produce 500,000 bottles of château wine. Our winegrowers bring in their grapes, we make the wine, stock it in vats, vineyard by vineyard, and each winegrower has his share.

"I'm surrounded by capable men working for me," the *maîtresse de maison* said. "A woman owner talks about her wine, represents her château, and, I believe, is looked on well. My business, what I've built and know about my wines, I learned on the job. I've an excellent oenologist and am surrounded by competent people. My son François runs the export side, and my daughters, our publicity and promotion."

Family life at the château is an integral part of the year's ritual. "La Chaize is the center of our family; my husband and I would come here every week. Now that I'm alone, I come for weekends. We all come down for the holidays as summer here is ideal—the climate, the beauty of the place, the green and the peace. We can swim if it's too hot, while the rest of the world drives on the roads. It's where we can all be together; for the grandchildren, La Chaize is a dreamworld.

"A château was always a very open place. Guests arrived with their baggage and servants and installed themselves for fifteen days or three weeks. I don't know how our ancestors managed. Today they stay less time. Gone, too, are the days when we left Paris at six in the evening, arriving here at two in the morning. Today the train takes a little over one hour.

"We receive our guests in a château ambience but nothing pompous. Our beautiful dining room holds elegant dinners, but always integrated as part of our family life, among friends. In the past, you never saw children in the house."

I recalled visiting La Chaize with Henri. "What a hospitable man!" Nicole Roussy de Sales declared. "You could arrive at Château des Granges at any hour. Henri would make us laugh. Life was a bit more Spartan over there.

A Beaujolais Vocabulary

la chamoure

la baguette, le bro	VINE SHOOT THAT REMAINS AFTER PRUNING
le barelet	SMALL BARREL
le barrique, le tonneau	BARREL
la benne	TUB FOR CARRYING GRAPES AT HARVESTTIME
le bistrot, le café	CAFÉ
le bois fendu	OAK PLANK USED TO MAKE BARRELS
la boutique	AREA OF THE CELLAR ONCE RESERVED FOR THE LOOM, WHEN WEAVING EARNED THE WINEGROWER A SUBSIDIARY INCOME
la calade	STONE FOUND NEAR VILLEFRANCHE
les caladois	RESIDENTS OF VILLEFRANCHE
le canton, le hameau	VILLAGE, HAMLET
la cassecroûte	EARLY MORNING SNACK
la chamoure	HARVESTERS' MEAL
le courtier	WINEBROKER
le Cru, les Crus	THE TEN BEAUJOLAIS GROWTHS (i.e. ST. AMOUR, FLEURIE, JULIÉNAS, ETC.)
la cuve	VAT
la cuvée	VAT FULL OF WINE

la benne

la cuvée

A Beaujolais Vocabulary

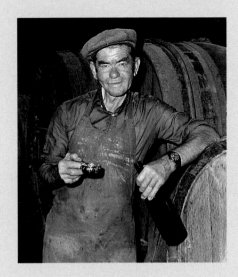

la dégustation

la grume

la dégustation	TASTING
l'échaudage	PROTECTION OF VINES FROM PYRALIS WORM USING CAULDRONS OF HOT WATER; INVENTED IN THE NINETEENTH CENTURY BY BENOIT RACLET OF ROMANÈCHE
fêtes des vendanges	HARVEST FESTIVAL
Fête des Deux Bouteilles	WINE FESTIVAL HELD IN VILLEFRANCHE IN DECEMBER, TO WHICH WINEGROWERS EACH BRING TWO BOTTLES OF THEIR NEW BEAUJOLAIS
les gresmottes	SMALL GRAPES LEFT ON VINES AFTER HARVESTING, AND THEN PICKED BY HARVESTERS FOR THEMSELVES
le grumage	BEAUJOLAIS TASTING CEREMONY
la grume	GRAPE
hectare	10,000 SQUARE METERS OR 2.47 ACRES—VINEYARD YIELD IS EXPRESSED IN HECTOLITERS PER HECTARE
hectoliter	26.42 U.S. GALLONS, 22.03 BR. IMP GALLONS
le mâchon	EARLY MORNING MEAL IN LYON AND BEAUJOLAIS
le maître de chai	CELLARMASTER

A Beaujolais Vocabulary

le marc — MASS OF SKINS AND SEEDS LEFT IN THE PRESS AFTER WINE HAS BEEN EXTRACTED; BRANDY DISTILLED FROM PRESSING IS CALLED *eau-de-vie de marc*, AND *marc d'Auvergne* IN THE AUVERGNE REGION

la mise en bouteilles — THE BOTTLING OF THE WINE

le négoce — WINE TRADE

le négociant — WINEMERCHANT

le paradis — FIRST WINE TASTED FROM THE VAT

la pièce — BARREL (215 LITERS, 225 LITERS IN BORDEAUX)

la pierre dorée — IN SOUTHERN BEAUJOLAIS, LOCAL BUILDING-STONE OF GOLDEN JURASSIC CHALK THAT REFLECTS SUNSHINE

le porte-vin — SHOP WHERE WINE IS SOLD "TO GO" (IN BORDEAUX *le porte-pot*)

le pot beaujolais — CLEAR GLASS BEAUJOLAIS WINE BOTTLE (46 CENTILITERS) USED AS A CARAFE IN CAFÉS

le pressoir — PRESS

le pressoir à dame — WOODEN PRESS

le proprietaire — OWNER, PROPRIETOR

le pressoir

la pierre dorée

le pressoir à dame

A Beaujolais Vocabulary

le tastevin

le vigneron

le raisin à dame	VERY SMALL, SWEET, TENDER GRAPES
le revole	END-OF-THE-HARVEST DINNER
le tastevin	SILVER TASTING CUP IN Beaujolais AND Burgundy
le terroir	SOIL
la veillée	TRADITIONAL EVENING GATHERING OF THE FAMILY
les vendanges	HARVEST
les vendangeurs	HARVESTERS
la vigne	VINE
le vigneron	WINEGROWER
le vignoble	VINEYARD
le vin	WINE
le vin de comptoir	CAFÉ WINE SERVED AT THE BAR OR COUNTER
le vin nouveau	THE NEW Beaujolais, OR *le Beaujolais nouveau*, READY FOR DRINKING ON THE THIRD Thursday OF November (ONCE CALLED *le vin primeur*)
le vin qui a fait ses Paques, vin de l'année	WINE OF THE YEAR, WHICH IS BOTTLED AFTER Easter
le viticulteur	WINEGROWER

les vendangeurs

Henri saw no reason to put in central heating, and when he did, he wouldn't hear of having it in the stairway.

"But what Henri did for Beaujolais was incredible. Knowing and loving his country so well, he saw it with a heroic vision. With a château of no great size, mayor of his village and looking after so many local problems, he was extraordinarily active. It wasn't just that he was such fun that they made him head of the Compagnons. He took them around the world. He worked for others. It is difficult to get such active people today to spend part of their time in the service of others."

We stood at the front door. The sun was coming out. "La Chaize is available for everyone: for the Compagnons, for *fêtes,* for the Crus, for *négociants* who want to show the château. There isn't much in the region of such dimensions. The underground cellar is spectacular, completely restored with vats from Burgundy. It brings back what our region once was: a dream of yesterday."

....

In a house in the vineyards, the winegrowers of Brouilly had prepared breakfast for me. Brouilly is a hill surrounded by six villages, little French villages of old churches with spires and houses around them, with between five and six hundred inhabitants each.

"Everyone knows everyone," began one of my hosts, Guy Brac de la Perrière of Château des Tours. "We get together for marriages, funerals, and the many public *fêtes.* A *fête* may be held for any reason, like the Fête of Pigs at Saint-Lager. Or the popular Fête du Paradis at harvesttime for the best juice from the press that we call *Le Paradis.* The new juice is very perfumed, very colored, and still a little sweet."

The wine of the year, the wine ready in spring, was on everyone's mind. "Everyone has learned to say, 'The New Beaujolais has arrived!' But the Beaujolais of the year is the wine our parents said had passed its Easter, *le vin qui a fait ses Pâques.* They taught us that at the end of winter a wine goes into a secondary fermentation and emerges with all its perfumes. So after Easter, the wine having been quiet in the cellars, the old winegrowers would decide to bottle it. For a wine like Brouilly, it's an error to bottle it too early."

"Usually we like to bottle with the moon descending," his neighbor added, "the first or second moon after Easter. We look at the moon to be sure the wine will be fine. My great-aunt one day received an order from her American importers to ship the wines immediately. She wrote back that it was not possible as the moon was not right to do the bottling. They must have thought they were dealing with some kind of witch!"

"A wine has the personality of the winemaker," said Brac de la Perrière. "The charm and appeal of our *appellations* are the many little vineyards, with enormous differences within one *appellation.* In Brouilly we are four hundred winegrowers. When you open the bottle, there's the charm of seeing a little of the winegrower in the bottle. Friends in Switzerland wrote me, 'This evening we opened a bottle and had a little moment in your cellar.'"

"Cooperatives represent about 20 percent of the production in Brouilly," said the president of the Brouilly. "More and more cooperatives are producing good wines. The more personalized wines are found at the winegrower. We try to capture the character of our land. Most of the vats in Beaujolais that our parents used before cement vats existed were originally vats for storing beer. They were imported from Germany and had to be reconditioned. Today when you go into a cellar full of big wood vats like at Château de la Chaize, with their warm color of wood, it's more rustic than cement. It's something else."

The growers keep a critical eye on each other's vineyard. "A good wine-grower, entering a vineyard, sees immediately if it has been well or badly pruned, if it has been too closely pruned. Pruning is important. After the big spring frosts, pruning can be most discouraging when you have to remake the vine, find new branches for buds to come on. The winegrower knows his vine just as he knows his dog. Each vine he prunes, he photographs it in his mind's eye, and hopes a lot. Hope begins here.

"The last year is always the best. Even when it has a little fault, it's good."

Breakfast over, the Beaujolais was brought in and poured, and our host's wife told us that for our breakfast the ham was home-cured, the bread was baked this morning, the butter was made by her mother. Looking out at the sea of vines, she said, "I was born in Beaujolais, but had never touched a vine until we married. We live here among the vines, and I work out there. I *touch* the vines!"

··········

Laid out under the trees in the park at Château des Granges was a picnic for twenty friends of the Rambuteau family. The smell of roasting floated over the garden. A whole lamb was turning on an open spit over glowing coals. The table was set with salad, cherries and raspberries from the garden, and carafes of Beaujolais.

Claude, Henri's son who now ran the château vineyards and cellars, was not there. I walked out to the vineyard and found him on his tractor. His bare, sun-drenched back glistened with sweat as he grappled with the plow. Above the roar of the engine, he invited me to meet some young winegrower neighbors with him next day. He was clearly still hurting from the loss of his father. I rejoined the family under the trees for their *déjeuner sur l'herbe.* Some weeks later I received a letter from Claude.

Mon Cher Michel,

My big winegrower's fingers, hardened by harvests, feel clumsy at machines like this typewriter! Work and emotions weigh heavy, but I'm optimistic! Papa, who had such warm feelings for you, seems more with me today than ever.

I remember those days when we young Rambuteaus learned our lessons at mealtimes at the long table in the kitchen, with Papa reciting the lives of the kings of France as if each was his own, the history of his seigneurs. More game than lesson, in less serious moments he told us of the more dissolute times of the Regencies and their mistresses. Since he read a lot, late into the night, lunch was often a summary of his nocturnal reading.

We learned to love the village where he was mayor for thirty years. "When I reach retirement or a respectable age," he would say, "I'll write its history." We

learned the Rambuteau passion for the forest. The family owned a forest well before we had vines. What Papa loved most was to walk around his trees a hundred times before deciding which tree to mark and cut down, or what to plant. Sometimes he took us for a sumptuous picnic at the shepherd's hut where we took you—sardines in olive oil, homemade saucisson, hard-boiled eggs, and country bread, washed down with our Beaujolais.

The wait for the harvest with the changes in weather demands all of a winegrower's strength, until that day when the wine is finally in the vats. Our harvesters used to come for the change in scenery and for human warmth. They worked, ate (thanks to Maman), drank, danced, laughed, and played. I still have Adrien, last of the colorful characters, who, for all his 72 years, never misses a harvest and sings lustily along with the champagne that marks the end of our harvesting. But today one minute of harvester's time costs me about 37 francs.

Cellarwork is so special, no school can teach it to you. I took the wine courses at Beaune, but I learned the real cellarwork with Papa and his cellar master, Dumoulin, a big character at Les Granges who died three months after Papa from the same illness. I learned from Papa the big lessons too, like listening to others and self-control. My first harvests and winemaking brought me much closer to him. We tasted the wines together in the cellar, a father ready to learn even in front of his son.

I think of our Beaujolais leaders who called their warhorse by the name of Integrity. Even in times of crisis such as we are going through today, I am confident there are people out there who buy and appreciate my wine.

At the château, preserving what Papa created, I hope soon to be able to increase our capacity with more vats for winemaking, storage, and bottling. I think of my children who one day I may send out into this exciting, passionate profession. As one of the young generation of winegrowers, I believe I shall come through, thanks to what Papa left me and what he taught me.

See you soon, *à bientôt,*

Claude de Rambuteau

· · · · · · · · · ·

The birth of a Beaujolais Cru, Appellation Saint-Amour, as told by the widow of its founder, Louis Dailly, is a little love story. She lives today with her daughter in the same gray stone house with high walls. They greeted me warmly and led me into their miniature cellar under the eaves in one corner of the courtyard.

Madame Dailly poured out her Beaujolais. "When war broke out in 1940, my husband and I left Paris and returned to the countryside. We'd been Parisians by adoption; I'm from Saint-Veran in the Mâcon region, my husband was from Saint-Amour. 'Working for others all my life,' he said, 'what I really want now is my own place.' We became *métayers* in a property here, every year paying the owner in wine or corn. It was May and we'd never worked a vineyard. The frosts came and, being Parisians, we knew nothing about all that."

"My father had been a waiter in a café in Paris," added the daughter; "my mother was a nurse."

"He was glad to be back in the country for his health," said the mother, "but I cried for days on end. We learned a lot and learned it by ourselves. We harvested a small crop and made the wine ourselves, advised by my brother in Juliénas. One night, returning home from dinner with my brother," Madame Dailly continued, "we could smell the new wine in the cellar and it smelled good. It was two in the morning and, to please my husband, I took them down to taste our new wine. Hearing them say 'I like your wine' was the start for us.

"The wines around here were only Appellation Beaujolais-Villages, but my husband was determined to obtain the *appellation* 'Saint-Amour.' From 1941 on, he spent each winter researching, listening to old winegrowers, checking documents they brought him, retracing the history of Saint-Amour. Louis Orizet, a Beaujolais historian, remembers him digging out royal edicts, church registers, marriage documents, donation inventories, inheritances, property sales, vineyard and geological surveys, vinification methods. Every Monday he left on his bicycle for town, returning on the Friday. I didn't see much of him. He assembled the winegrowers of Saint-Amour and began the syndicat. Finally, he assembled the most voluminous dossier the INAO had ever seen on its desks, and Saint-Amour was officially awarded its *appellation* as *Cru*.

"My Louis was father of the Cru Saint-Amour; without him, we would still be Beaujolais-Villages. Yet at what a price; the pressure of work and tension killed him. But my vines, my beautiful noble ladies, are always there, holding me, encouraging me, whispering encouragement to me."

THE NÉGOCIANT'S STORY

*The autumn heat prepares us for the harvest. The vines are heavy with grapes, the sound of wine is in the vats, the songs of the girls harvesting carries an air of festivities, **la fête.** The useful join hands with the agreeable. Each morning the veil of mist is lifted by the sun like a theater curtain to reveal this spectacle.*

—JEAN-JACQUES ROUSSEAU

In Rousseau's day it was fashionable for aristocracy—perhaps the Princess of Condé, the Duke of Croy, and the Duchess of Bourbon—to call a halt from their promenades and enter a farm, sit down at the table, and share the country folks' meal of black bread, eggs, and cream.

The modern aristocracy in the wine trade, the wine merchants, are to be found each September at harvesttime out visiting the cellars of the wine-growers, selecting the best vats of wine that they will buy from the new vintage as it comes into the pressing house from the vineyards. Ninety percent of the wine made at the cooperatives in Beaujolais is sold to the wine merchants, the *négociants.* Sometimes the wine merchant buys direct from the wine-

grower, sometimes he buys through a winebroker or wine commissioner, who act as middlemen. These professions are institutions, existing in Beaujolais as in Burgundy and Bordeaux since time immemorial. The wine merchants bring the wines they buy into their own cellars and nurture them there, until they are ready for the assembling of the vats, the *assemblage,* and bottling. Some wine merchants call themselves *négociants-élèveurs,* since their work is the careful bringing up, *élèvage,* of the wines from the vat until they are ready to drink.

From Growth to Growth, cellar to cellar, the *négociant* goes, notebook in hand, as each winegrower goes to his vat, draws a sample in a *tastevin,* offers his wine for tasting, and waits. I remembered my days with Emile Peynaud in Bordeaux at harvesttime, going from château to château, as he advised each owner on the winemaking.

"It's more difficult in Beaujolais," said the *négociant* Georges Duboeuf. "Everything happens so fast. I visit a cellar at least ten times during harvest. The winegrower must follow my instructions to the letter. In our lab at the winery, we analyze their wines — about two hundred wines a day after harvesting begins."

Two winebrokers had brought us here. Duboeuf insists on tasting for himself in the cellars all wines recommended by brokers. "This morning I visited some dozen cellars, starting at four in the morning. It's been like that since harvesting began, and every year the same."

The winegrower is allowed to produce fifty hectoliters of Nouveau wine per hectare. The rest of his wine is restrained by law to remain in the cellar, to be released after December 15 as the wine of the year.

The next Nouveau we tasted, the *négociant* had tasted once before. "At each tasting I note its evolution. Over the years, I remember everything that happens in each cellar I visit. We taste vat by vat, then blind-taste samples back at the lab, not knowing where the wines come from. We reanalyze, review our decisions, and finally decide what we'll buy."

The first cellar was a mixture of old wood and new stainless steel vats. The *négociant* tasted, said nothing.

"Monsieur," the winegrower addressed him with respect, "our malolactic fermentation was so slow finishing, I was scared. We spent ages this year in the vats cleaning them out, but the yeasts were still around. Like last year, we began harvesting late."

2. Les Vendanges. — Groupe de Vendangeurs.

F. GUILLARD, Distilleries et Vignobles, à Frontenas (Rhône). - Le Personnel

Les VENDANGES — Repas des Vendangeurs

LÉMONON-DUCOTÉ ÉDIT MACON

"Yes, but you need only a little bacteria in the vats, and they're off!" the *négociant* said calmly. "With over five hundred yeasts on the market, you must take care which one you use. Yesterday I tasted several vats, each using a different yeast. The difference was enormous. Yeast No. 71B seems to work well for Nouveau wines, but it also depends on the year. The 71B consumes a lot of the acid, so in years with little acidity, we use another yeast. Everyone should use the yeast best suited to his winemaking. Come to our lab tomorrow and they'll tell you more."

"I've heard of a yeast that produces extraordinary perfumes of banana," said the winegrower.

"If you smell bananas coming from the grape when the malolactic fermentation starts, you know you've missed out making a good wine," Duboeuf replied. Later he told me that that winegrower's problems had come from his having started harvesting too late. "There are effective products to clean vats well, but starting so late, the bacteria are all around."

At the next cellar, the wine pleased. "We must be on our way, but my colleagues here, the *courtiers,* will be by tomorrow for samples—half bottles of each vat, especially vat number seven that I just tasted. Remarkable wine."

"Okay for the seven," said the owner, pleased, "and you'll tell me what you need."

Even when a *négociant* looks happy he usually sounds wary. "This year, his wines are less perfumed, less fat, less round, as the grapes suffered much more from heat than last year. One evening in early September, it was incredible to see the vines looking so thirsty, bowed down and weak, through lack of water. It was as if they were really crying out for water, really afraid of heat. Then came the September rains, and the volume increased. If we hadn't had the rains, who knows what wines we'd have made? Despite suffering from drought and rains, this year's wines will be ranked among the good vintages."

At the next cellar, the owner inquired how his colleagues in other regions were faring. He was told that the south of Beaujolais was harvesting with the same weather, very hot for the season, without a drop of rain in fifteen days. Such marvelous weather increased the volume, and the wines were well balanced.

"Would you call ours a late harvest?" the winegrower asked.

"Not at all. We'll all be finishing around October 10, whereas some years we start harvesting around then. They're always later in southern Beaujolais, due to altitude, soil, and so many things. The harvest always starts first up here. I see the first troops of harvesters here, the first flowering of the vines, too."

The next cellar, no larger than a one-car garage, was built in the seventeenth century. Duboeuf had found what he'd been looking for. He passed me his *tastevin*. "Taste this. The wine is beautiful, frank, and firm. I like it. It's from your old vines?"

"Yes, monsieur."

"The second vat tastes less good than when I was here last week. We'll take a half bottle from each vat and let you know how the *malo* is progressing. How much do you have as Nouveau?"

"The lot," replied the owner, happy. "All I ask is to sell you everything. Choose what you wish, at the current market price, whatever that is. As long as I don't get left with wine on my hands at the end of the year."

They shook hands. Back in the car, Duboeuf confided to me, "One year I found certain tastes in his wine that weren't right. We could find no explanation. I called up the labs in Bordeaux, Toulouse, Montpellier, Dijon, even called Professor Puisais, the oenologist. No one had an answer. 'It's too complicated,' they all said. They made more tests. Nothing. Then it disappeared during the winemaking. Some days it's there, some days it's not. After the wine has been racked, in my opinion, it'll disappear. The vines were well washed by the rains this year."

The next winemaker appeared to be eighteen years old but clearly knew his winemaking. "*Impeccable,*" declared Duboeuf, his nose deep in the glass.

On the way home, Duboeuf gave the *négociant*'s view of the vintage. "A good vintage, very good, depending on the region, but it's early for a global judgment. I've only tasted the Beaujolais, Beaujolais-Villages, and a few of the Crus. We know it's an abundant harvest, larger in volume than last year's. No green grapes, good ripe grapes, no rot, so the wines are well balanced. Perhaps not totally to my taste—a little too firm, a little too tannic, too hard, but surely wines to stand up well and keep well.

"You saw how the pressing houses even smelled good. You were smelling successful winemaking, healthy wines without problems. Last year was an

exceptional vintage, marvelous from every angle, with the Beaujolais Growths sure to last five or ten years. The Beaujolais-Villages were marvelous too."

....

In Côtes de Brouilly I discussed with a group of winegrowers the tension and anticipation that brings them together every year at this time. Prior to the harvest starting, they are called by the Union Interprofessionnel in Villefranche for the pre-harvest conference.

"Some twelve hundred of us winegrowers gather together in the cellars at the Cuvage of Lacenas," said one winegrower. "I like to go because it warms us up."

"We follow the union's technical instructions," one of his colleagues went

on. "They remind us about vat temperatures, tell us the strong and weak points of the vintage, the conditions in the vineyard. It gives us faith to do the best possible."

I asked the group if they saw much of each other at harvesttime. "Very little. Before the harvest we meet often. When the harvest is over, we exchange our wines and taste them. During the harvest, one's concentrated on one's work. Everyone has his own way of making his wine. Harvesttime is a very intense moment. We aren't looking for any distraction."

In difficult years, I asked, do winegrowers meet and discuss their problems?

"If the winemaking is going badly, we go to our neighbor to see how it's going with him. We don't have secrets, and that's not just in Beaujolais."

Two of the group were also *négociants,* and a key moment in the *négociant*'s work is the *assemblage.*

"The *assemblage* is when it becomes really interesting," said one of the *négociants.* "A little vat of exceptional quality can dominate the whole batch of wines that we are trying to assemble. Then there are the wines that don't show themselves straightaway."

"I know what I'm looking for," said his colleague. "When the wines are still young and in the process of finishing, you must taste them every day, as wines change constantly. One tries to draw out the quintessence of what one has. What is difficult is that once the *assemblage* is done, it's done.

"These *assemblages* are the strength of some *négociants* who are able to make good *assemblages* with the different wines they buy. At harvesttime we know what has to be done. The vat may guide us and we do our best. But most of the time, nature is the mistress who decides."

When they find the wine they want, is it a good moment?

"Of course, but one's never really sure," a winegrower replied. "When I find the wine, I go back to the house with some samples, taste them again in a blind tasting, taste them with my wife, and again at mealtime. Then I put them aside, forget them, and later start all over again. I can be half a day in my cellar tasting, thinking, trying again and again. Alone. I don't like questions while I'm working on selecting my wine. I'm impassioned, concentrating on my responsibility."

....

Georges Paquet, the *négociant,* works and lives in the village of Le Perréon, in the valley below Vaux-en-Beaujolais. The hillsides around his winery are woven in a patchwork of small vineyards.

"The vineyards are man-size," said Georges Paquet. "We say around here that a man cannot work a fifty-hectare vineyard. Family-size means a vineyard for father with son and family to work. They need four or five hectares, for one simple reason: any larger, they would need a worker, making it no longer family-size. With my secateurs I can prune five or six hundred of my ten thousand vines a day. When the weather is bad, I don't work. As each piece of a vineyard is about 2,500 vines, the winegrower needs four or five hectares. He begins pruning around November 15 to December 15, then January 15 to February 15 or at latest, March 15. It is the winegrower himself who prunes his vines, no one else. A worker will do many other vineyard jobs, but he alone is the one, secateurs in hand, who decides the vineyard yield."

The Paquet family began in 1762 as agricultural workers in the region with a few vines. To survive the difficult years, they also raised a large herd of cattle. Some of the family became winegrowers, others became wine brokers, others became carters.

"My grandfather had eighteen horses," Paquet recalled. "It was a sight to see the carts loaded with barrels four high, leaving for the bistros in Lyon. We lost all that in the last war. Starting again, my father and I decided to buy vines so as to have our own wine. We did excellent business selling to bistros. For many years they only had Beaujolais as the popular red wine. When Beaujolais began to conquer Paris and the export markets, the prices went up and the worker could no longer afford a *pot* of Beaujolais.

"That convinced us to become *négociants* in 1948 and buy other wines. Never too late to start, I took my suitcase and went selling our wines for export. Our best clients in Lyon went through a 215-liter barrel of wine a day. Since these bistros were open 365 days of the year, we would sell them three hundred barrels a year. We'd buy several whole cellars at a time, and the bistro owners came with us to the winegrower to select their wine. But these bistros have practically disappeared; perhaps only a dozen of them are left in Lyon today."

His family winery in the hills is what Georges Paquet calls traditional size. "We're the size we are because we like to sleep at night."

Before harvest starts, like other *négociants* he is out visiting the winegrowers he will buy from, advising them on the new vintage. "We tell them if the wine will need more or less vatting, more aromas, or a little more structure. The winegrower listens to the one who will buy his wine."

Georges Paquet believes strongly in the simple Appellation Beaujolais wines. "For the bistro-style restaurateur they should still be one of his best-selling wines. A Beaujolais-Villages will stay a little longer in the mouth and can be kept a little longer in the cellar. On a hot day, I go down into my cellar which is at twelve degrees and bring up, not a rosé, but a young cool bottle of Beaujolais, to serve with a barbecued steak."

The *négociant*'s image of the cool of a cellar reminded me of one of the writer Colette's visits to Beaujolais in the summer of 1948. In a cellar, the cellar master offered his illustrious but aged guest some wine in a silver *tastevin*. "There, madame, you are tasting a perfect '47," he told her, "but come back again and visit us when our '48 is ready. It will rival this one." Later Colette wrote in her journal, "Come back! How easy and probable the words sounded when one is in a cellar, that cool grotto that keeps the heat out, and one had on one's lips the cold edge of a cup full of wine."

· · · · · · · · · ·

always seemed to end up in Beaujeu. One of the old firms in town, the Maison Tête, has cellars just above in the village called Les Dépôts. Grandfather Tête began in 1921 at Les Dépôts. His son Louis and grandson Jean Tête were both born here.

"Everyone would go to the cafés in Beaujeu," said Jean Tête as we sat and tasted in the cellar of one of his winegrowers, "because at home the children would be screaming, the kitchen was small, it was uncomfortable. They went to the café where they felt comfortable, among friends."

"People spent time in the cafés," the winegrower recalled. "They came down from the mountain, there were markets and fairs, and no cars. We used to go to dances in the hills. Fifty years ago, the mountains were all forests."

"Gradually the mountain farms are disappearing," said Jean Tête. "They no longer pay. The farm people had six or seven cows, three or four goats, several sheep, two or three pigs. They made their own *charcuterie* and bread. They needed to buy little—some wine when they felt like it, some groceries. They made oil with the walnuts. Some still bring their nuts down and take back a liter of oil. We have the only oil manufacturer in the region at Beaujeu. Once Beaujeu was known for its tanneries, too."

As we left the cellar, Tête explained, "We've been buying his wine for years. Even when it pleases us a little less, we manage to sell it. Unlike the *négociants* who work through wine brokers, we buy directly. As the one who does the buying in our firm, I know all the winegrowers around. I'm their friend. Some evenings, if I pass by around five or six, I look in and drink a glass of wine with them. Another winegrower passes by, we become three. Another and another, we talk and the ambience grows."

The next winegrower had retired, but not retired from tasting in the cellar. His parents started the vineyard and he began working for his father without pay. "I've been selling my wines to Monsieur Tête for the past ten years. The wine brokers know, so they don't come here anymore."

Jean Tête, who is younger, told how he began. "My first years were catastrophic," he said. "The wine wasn't selling, and though 1952 was normal, in '53 we had the frost. It was also the year I got married—catastrophic!"

I asked him how they work together, *négociant* and winegrower.

"Once the wine is in the vats, we know what we have. We discuss price, but one mustn't come on too strong just then. He has to sell his wine at the best

Beaujolais Wine Tasting Cellars
Open to the Public

La Maison du Beaujolais, *Saint-Jean-d'Ardieres*

La Terrasse des Beaujolais, *Pommiers*

Le Temple de Bacchus, *Beaujeu*

Le Cadole du Char a Boeufs, *Chasselas*

Le Pavillon des Pierres Dorées, *Chatillon-d'Azergues*

Le Cellier du Babouin, *Chazay d'Azergues*

Le Caveau des Voutes, *Cogny*

Le Caveau des Vignerons, *Fleurie*

Le Cellier de la Vieille Eglise, *Juliénas*

Le Caveau de Jullié, *Jullié*

Le Relais Beaujolais-Maconnais, *Leynes*

Le Caveau du Moulin-à-Vent, *Romanèche-Thorins*

Le Caveau de l'Union des Viticulteurs du Moulin-à-Vent, *Romanèche*

La Tasse du Chapitre, *Salles*

Le Caveau du Cru Saint-Amour, *Saint-Amour*

Le Refuge des Pierres Dorées, *Saint-Jean-des-Vignes*

Le Cuvage des Brouilly, *Saint-Lager*

Le Caveau de l'Union des Viticulteurs de Saint-Verand, *Saint-Verand*

Le Caveau de Clochemerle, *Vaux-en-Beaujolais*

Le Caveau des Morgon, *Villié-Morgon*

Tasting cellars are also located in the following cooperatives: *Bully, Chiroubles, Fleurie, Gleizé, Juliénas, Lachassagne, Bois d'Oignt, Letra, Le Perréon, Saint-Etienne-des-Oullières, Saint-Laurent-d'Oignt, Saint-Verand, and Theizé.*

price possible and earn a living. It has to be good for me, too. I buy all his cellar of wine. If one year I pay a little less for his wine, the next year I up the price for him. If I paid a little more one year and it didn't sell so well, next year I pay a little less. It balances out. There are no risks, on either side."

"I can't complain too much," said the winegrower. "He pays pretty well, too. We also hunt together!"

"We had no market price last year," Tête went on. "You bought a wine in March, a month later it cost two hundred francs less. Very painful for everyone as no one was buying. This year there is buying because we're sure about prices; there are no risks."

The good old days are within living memory. "One of the big cafés of Lyon, Hours, we'd sell a hundred barrels at a time," recalled Jean Tête. "Loading the carts at the winegrower took all day and made the winegrower so happy that he paid for a big meal to celebrate. Today, the cistern truck is loaded with two hundred hectos in an hour, and it is gone. They were true café owners, true wine lovers. Old Hours didn't just serve his wine. If something wasn't right with the wine, he told the customer and went back down into his cellar for a new bottle. The cafés rivaled each other. Customers made a tour of them as soon as the Nouveau arrived, to find out where the best Nouveau in town was."

Café life is a common thread running through Beaujolais. "There was an extraordinary ambience in these cafés," said Jean Tête with enthusiasm. "Big businesses had their headquarters in the center of Lyon, so you had the president of a company, his office clerk or a taxi driver, people from totally different social backgrounds, talking and drinking at the tables. There was a fantastic exchange and ambience. We live so differently today. Cafés have become sad places. Doctors are grouped over there, workers over there. It's no longer fun. Once in Beaujeu there were forty cafés full of people. When you offered a *pot,* it was good, it was Beaujolais. Today, it may be some table wine or other."

"You've been here all your life?" I asked the old winegrower.

"Where else?" he replied. "They say if one stays in one place, one becomes implanted. It's too late to make a change."

Beaujeu once had train service with fourteen passenger trains a day. Then it slowed down to four, then five years ago it stopped completely, with just one freight train a day.

"There was a little train called *le tacot,*" recalled Jean Tête, "that followed the road by our village, over viaducts, twisting around the mountain. My grandmother lived on the mountain, so we'd take it to see her. The train would stop and the guard would get down and drink a *pot* of Beaujolais with his friends."

· · · · · · · · · ·

The *négociant*'s visit to his winegrower depends on a certain trust built up over the years. "I go to the cellar, seldom to the house, to sign the contract," Duboeuf explained back in his own cellars in the village of Romanèche-Thorins, "as generally everything takes place in the cellar. First, we discuss winemaking: what to do, which yeasts to use, drawing on experience and my visits to other winegrowers who have begun winemaking. Second, we start talking price. We taste the vats and talk about everything under the sun. Sometimes his wife joins us. One has to know one's winegrower well.

"The best Beaujolais-Villages are always an assembling of wines. The best Moulin-à-Vent, raised in oak barrels, is an *assemblage.* The *appellation* 'Beaujolais-Villages' applies to thirty-eight villages," he explained, "with wines that give fruit, elegance, and finesse. A Beaujolais-Villages from Le Perréon gives body, a Beaujolais-Villages from Bois-d'Oignt gives fat and roundness, a Beaujolais-Villages from Saint-Etienne-la-Varenne or Saint-Etienne-les-Oullières gives tenderness, another gives elegance. The marriage of all that is the *négociant*'s work: the nurturing and *assemblage* of the wine."

His profession, and what he called his passion, is spending two hours a day, from 11 to noon and from 5:30 to 6:30 in the evening, tasting forty samples a day. In the buying season, October through January, he tastes three hundred samples a day over three months. "It would be easier if all winegrowers produced the same wine," he said, "but that is not so. There are enormous differences between them.

"Once a year we *négociants* have three or four months to do our market, and we must do it well. Good vats of wine are like good produce a chef searches for at the market; if you're not there early, they're gone.

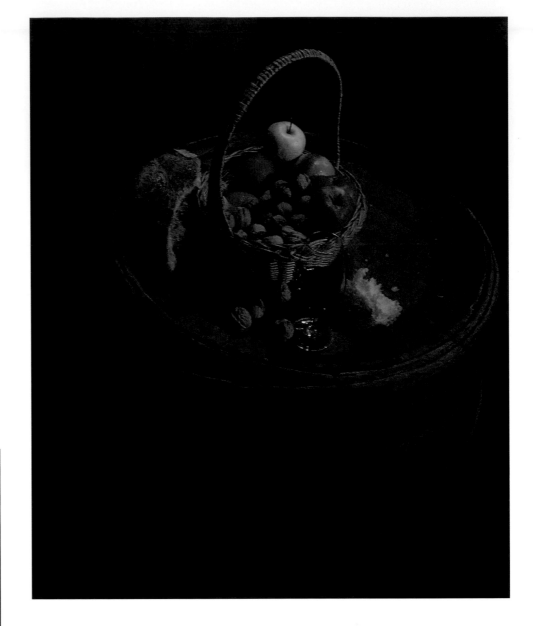

"Later, like the chef with his produce from the market, we must make the right *assemblage* with the vats of wine we have bought. Each of us has his own style of winemaking."

Emile Peynaud, the great Bordeaux oenologist and winemaker, said that when the wine he makes pleases him, he knows it will please others.

"I like a certain style of wine," said Duboeuf, "but I am not sure it will please everyone. Some may criticize it."

THE "GRAND DÉPART" AND CELEBRATION

The third Thursday in November, zero hour, one minute past midnight. The trucks that have been revving up their motors in the cellar yards sail forth into the night like ships. With five million cases of Beaujolais Nouveau—sixty million bottles—loaded aboard, they speed through the sleeping villages en route to Paris. One million of the cases will travel on by air or by ship to all points of the compass.

This has been the scenario for Beaujolais Nouveau for the past quarter century. The first taste has become a race to the finish, in bottle, barrel, or container, by balloon, Concorde jet, helicopter, Hovercraft, motorcycle, racing car, rickshaw, sherpa, elephant, camel, or by foot.

Each year Paris awakes to find the bistros, restaurants, and stores hung with banners proclaiming the good news: "*Le Beaujolais Nouveau est arrivé!*" The New Beaujolais has arrived!

"Today's our big Beaujolais Nouveau Day," declared Louis Prin, owner of the restaurant Ma Bourgogne on Boulevard Haussmann, and president of the group of the best Beaujolais restaurants in Paris, Les Meilleurs Pots du Beaujolais. "Though you don't have to be a Meilleur Pot to celebrate the ideal wine to serve at the bar, to drink just as it is, without having to eat. By this

evening, everyone in the neighborhood will be in here to taste the new Beaujolais."

The waiters brought up bottles from the underground cellar. I followed Monsieur Prin through a trap door and down steep steps leading to a vaulted cellar lined with barrels. He tapped a barrel. "Twice a year, in early November for the Nouveau wine and in January for the wine of the Crus, I and some colleagues go down to Beaujolais to taste and select our wine. I buy part of the wine in barrels as we bottle it ourselves down here, to last us through July. I reserve another vat that my winegrower bottles in Beaujolais, to last us to the end of the year.

"Beaujolais is best when it protects its youth, so we must bottle it young. The New Beaujolais, just arrived by truck, sparkles with its carbonic gas and tastes so fresh in the mouth. If I don't use conical corks, they'll jump out of the bottle. We still put the Beaujolais bottle, *le pot,* on the table. The customer doesn't have to finish the bottle. Or they can ask us for another bottle and drink half the bottle. They can drink and pay only for what they drink."

His restaurant is the home of the Académie Rabelais. "We hold our academy's annual dinners either here or every two years in the Beaujolais with Gerard Canard and the Compagnons du Beaujolais. Many illustrious figures of theater, cinema, literature, and politics have been members.

"We also have the Francs Mâchons," Louis Prin continued, "a group begun down in Lyon and Beaujolais in honor of their traditional early morning snack, *le mâchon.* They meet a dozen times a year, at two in the morning. The Compagnons hold two events, called *devoirs,* here during the year. We celebrated the Académie Rabelais's thirtieth anniversary with six hundred guests. On the pavements outside, in the corridors and courtyard of the building, I set out trees and tents and Beaujolais everywhere. We played bowls, with bales of straw and sand along the Boulevard Haussmann. Passersby were invited to have a glass of Beaujolais, free! I always hope a van of police will draw up and we can invite them in, too. I invite the mayor; I invite everyone. Tomorrow we're holding a bowling party on the Esplanade of Les Invalides to celebrate the arrival of the Nouveau, and I'll set up a buffet with Beaujolais. Come and join us."

....

La Mère Brazier

"The late Mère Brazier," says Paul Bocuse, "stands as a symbol of the great culinary tradition of Lyon. Thanks to her, the great French food critic Curnonsky named our city The 'World Capitol of Gastronomy.'" Bocuse began working for Mère Brazier as a kitchen helper in 1946, at the age of twenty-one. "Work was everything: we learned how to milk the cows and feed the pigs every night with leftovers from the meals. We even made our own electricity. Everyone shared in the laundry, ironing, gardening, cleaning, work in the winecellar…there were no specialists. Though she shouted at us from morning to night, we respected her.

"Her menus varied little but were always perfect. The *Poularde de Bresse* on my menu today is from her restaurant, where we cooked fifty of them each Sunday. They talk of *nouvelle cuisine* today, but it does not mean that much. There are two kinds of cuisine: good and bad. Her cuisine was simple and honest, demanding without any pretension."

La Mère Richard restaurant on rue Royale in Lyon, is run today by her daughter Carmen Brazier and granddaughter, Jacotte. The à la carte menu preserves the dishes—and the quality of Beaujolais—that have made its reputation since 1921.

France's second city, Lyon, is only fifty kilometers from Beaujolais by road as the horse and winecart trundled. Lyon was for several centuries the wine's principal market, while the city's thriving silk trade supported a multitude of restaurants and bustling bistros and cafés.

Lyon created the *mâchon,* an early morning snack once popular among the silk executives; today it is the time to meet the chefs after they have been to the market. Paul Bocuse, the world-renowned chef, is a regular at the Lyon market. Over a *mâchon,* he drew a map on the paper tablecloth, describing Lyon as the larder of France. "Starting to the north, you have the wines of Beaujolais," he began, "and the market gardens of the valley of the Saône. Further north you have Burgundy and its wines; to the northeast, the Dombes region with its Bresse chickens, game, and freshwater fish—carp, perch, and pike. East to Lake Annecy with trout and small lake fish; lower down, the Drôme region with ducks and geese; south to the Rhône valley with more vineyards and fruit; and to the west, the Charolais region and its beef. Surrounded by so much quality produce, the Lyon people have become very demanding *gourmands.* No other region has seven three-star restaurants within one hundred kilometers of each other."

Paul has always been a strong supporter of the Lyon market, though the modern building lacks the ambience of the old market. "I learned that it's important to go to the market every day to see the produce, have contact with the producers. There's good cuisine in Lyon because of the good produce. Without it, there cannot be good cuisine. We chefs are like big families. Restaurateurs like the Mère Brazier have been like mothers to the young chefs.

"Our friends at the market are all people of the soil. Like René Besson, whom we call Bobosse, from Vaux, who has learned to give pride of place to produce from the land with his own good *saucissons, andouillettes, pâtés,* and *terrines.* Bobosse is the image of a good Lyon producer. Naturally he likes to eat and drink the Beaujolais. It's part of the art of living. Another like him at the market is the Mère Richard and her cheeses from the farms. It would be inconceivable not to visit Madame Richard and Bobosse when I go to the market."

The Wednesday morning *mâchon* is when the chefs gather and talk over a dozen oysters, a sausage, a steaming bowl of local tripe stew, and a mutton-foot salad, washed down with freshly chilled Beaujolais.

On the Menu: Regional Specialties

andouillettes	small pork sausages
boudin aux pommes	blood sausage (pork) with apples
bouillon gras	vegetable and meat soup
bugnes	Lyon-style fritters
chapon roti aux marrons	roast capon with chestnuts
civet de lièvre, de cevreuil, de sanglier	stew of hare, roe deer, boar
coq au vin	chicken cooked in wine
coq au Fleurie	chicken cooked in Fleurie wine
friture de goujons	deepfried miniature lake fish
fromage blanc	fresh farmer's cheese
gigot de mouton braisé lyonnaise	lamb with garlic cooked in a cocotte (earthenware pot)
gratinée lyonnaise	Lyon-style onion soup
gratin de cardons à la moelle	cardoons and bone marrow gratin
gras-double à la lyonnaise	Lyon-style honeycomb tripe
cervelle de canut	fresh herbed cheese
poires à la beaujolais	pears in Beaujolais
poularde aux écrevisses	hen with crayfish
poulet à la crème	chicken in cream sauce

On the Menu: Regional Specialties

poulet à l'ail	chicken with garlic
pot-au-feu	beef stew
ragout de mouton au Beaujolais	lamb stew cooked in Beaujolais
rosette	sausage eaten with the Beaujolais of the year
sabaudet	pot-bellied sausage stuffed with pork rind and jowls, well cooked in bouillon, and served with lentils
salade de pieds de mouton	mutton-foot salad
salade de pommes de terre et saucisson pistache	potato and pistachio sausage salad
saladier lyonnaise	dandelion green, bacon, herring, anchovy, and crouton salad
saucisson brioche	sausage cooked in buttery, egg-enriched yeast bread
soupe aux chou	cabbage soup
soupe au potiron	pumpkin or gourd soup
tablier de sapeur	local tripe stew
tête de veau	rolled poached veal's head
volaille de Bresse à la broche	chicken roasted on a spit

"Some start their *mâchon* about seven o'clock," said Paul. "For those who are up at two a.m. to go to the market, seven is like midday for them. Others *mâchon* at eight, nine, or ten. The company presidents, the late ones, eat at eleven. The *mâchon* is the best time of the day, when you can hear all the stories which end up being the truth in a matter of a few years."

....

Wooden Leg Soup

This is an old Lyon recipe given to Paul Bocuse many years ago by the late Henry Clos-Jouve, President of the Academie Rabelais, a food society renowned for its ambiance and fine dinners in the restaurants of Lyon and Paris. "It's really an enormous *pot au feu*, or stew," explains Bocuse. "First, you soak a fine loin of beef in cold water, adding salt, onions, herbs, and anything else on hand to give flavor, and simmer gently in a very large pot, skimming until the soup is clear. Add leeks, turnips, celery, veal shins, pork shoulder, game, pieces of turkey, leg of lamb, and a rump of beef. Half an hour before serving, add a couple of large chickens followed, a few minutes later, by some pork sausages generously stuffed with truffles and pistachio nuts. Once cooked, carry in the soup with a shin bone laid across the pot to symbolize the Soup with a Wooden Leg. It was a big favorite in Lyon, and I still serve it in my restaurant as *La Soupe à la Jambe de Bois.*"

Chicken with
Truffles à la Mère Brazier
POULARDE DE BRESSE TRUFFÉE MERE BRAZIER

The secret of this easy recipe is in the quality of the chicken, ideally from the Dombes, across the river from Beaujolais.

   1 *Bresse chicken (approx. 4lbs.)*
   1 *truffle*
  ¼ *lb. carrots*
   1 *bouquet garni*
       mustard, cornichons, griotte cherries in vinegar,
       and sea salt

Slice the truffle into slivers about a quarter of an inch thick and slip them under the skin of the chicken around the breast, and under each thigh. Wrap tightly in muslin, and truss. Put carrots and bouquet garni in a large pot half full of water, bring to a boil, add chicken, and simmer slowly (about 45 minutes for a 4lb. chicken). Allow to sit in its bouillon for 30 minutes before serving. Serve chicken with vegetables, bouquet garni, mustard, cornichons, etc. and the Beaujolais of the year.

Spring in Beaujolais. The winegrowers are once more out visiting neighbors, tasting their own and their colleagues' wines. The late Alexis Lichine called the little world of Beaujolais "France's richest mine of great peasant wine folklore, celebrating the humor, hard work and *joie de vivre* of its people. . . . If ever winemakers were blessed, it is the growers of Beaujolais."

Good times and bad, year in, year out, that sense of conviviality continues. Storms on the horizon, rising costs on the grapevine and in the cellar, nothing will change tradition, father to son; his Beaujolais in the cellar is for tasting in good company. One is always welcome.

"Come back when we are celebrating one of our two big annual *fêtes,* when we're assembled at the table with good wines and food," Henri de Rambuteau advised me on my first time in Beaujolais. "Visit us the first weekend of December, when we hold in Villefranche the *Fête des Deux Bouteilles,* as everyone goes with two bottles under his arm. There's an enormous banquet; you can imagine how much is drunk. After the banquet we go over to the large sportsdrome where they've specially covered the ground with sawdust so we can taste and spit out the wines competing in the Paradise Cup. A superb event. I always go with a small group of my generation, as I'm one of the old ones! Some twenty of us, if one of us wins the Cup, usually we all dine together to celebrate and wash down the victory. Each one pays for the champagne, which costs a lot. If we haven't won, we all dine together to console ourselves, which is just as expensive." He laughed. "Our wives never see us back before three in the morning."

The other big festival day is in January, Saint Vincent's Day, the patron saint of winegrowers. Henri described the scene. "They all invite their friends to a fantastic banquet and take it in turn to be Vincent. When you're Vincent, you invite all your friends which is very expensive. Since I'm mayor of the village, it would be incompatible for me to be Vincent. It's equally inconceivable that I pay for my dinner. So I'm obliged to wait until the end of the meal when I have to pay for two or three bottles of champagne—which is much more expensive. I'm condemned to sit until two or three in the morning and always, always, I'm seated next to Monsieur le Curé.

"The ladies are invited to this banquet. The whole family comes. We sit down about midday, a course is served about every hour, all day. After dessert,

Les Compagnons du Beaujolais

This solemn oath is sworn by each new *Compagnon*, beneath a wooden statue of St. Vincent.

"I swear before St. Vincent to lead the life of a faithful, free *Compagnon du Beaujolais*. I swear to love our countryside, uphold its traditions of hospitality, wisdom, and good humor; to share with others the beauty of the land, its ancient churches and châteaux that bear witness to a past enriched by the spirit of its builders and artisans; to encourage the appreciation of the wine from our vines and, finally, to honor the good men of the soil—our wine-growers—whose good work forges the prosperity and just reward for our land and home, the Beaujolais."

about 5 p.m., there's a pause, *le trou de milieu*. Everyone stops and I always wondered why. In fact they go off to milk the cows and return to sit down again about seven, bringing with them some more friends. Since they've also visited their own cellars, the ambience is now getting very Beaujolais. Late into the night each one gets up to sing a song or tell a story. I have my story to tell. You mustn't surprise them. They don't appreciate a new story."

....

One place, Vaux-en-Beaujolais, the little village in the hills with its view of Mont Blanc on a clear day, has been haunting this story since my first day in Beaujolais. "Whenever I return from a trip, I don't go straight home," Bobosse told me the first time I drove to Vaux with him. "I take the car and drive into the Beaujolais. I'm so madly in love with my Beaujolais! I know all the little roads that lead to my Vaux!" Driving to Vaux that day, Bobosse took each bend in the road as if he were on Le Mans racetrack. "That's my best friend's house with the pond," he cried across to me. "I brought him ducks from my pond, but when I got home the ducks had flown back home, too!" One more bend and Vaux appeared above us, its houses clinging to the hillside. Bobosse exclaimed, "I want my ashes laid here, halfway between Vaux and neighboring Le Perréon. I grew up here," declared Bobosse proudly. "It's the heart of Beaujolais!"

Each time I visit Beaujolais, I too need one more time in Vaux. On a recent trip in winter, the gas lamps hanging from the houses up the one narrow street gave a golden aura to the village. Vaux is renamed Clochemerle in the Gabriel Chevalier novel *Clochemerle* that has become a classic of French comic literature.

A faded sky blue poster on the wall opposite the mayor's office announced last summer's *fête*. In Chevalier's day, on the eve of a *fête,* every house in the village of Clochemerle would be stirred into action, "with a profusion of chickens prepared the night before, rabbits in their marinades for the past forty-eight hours, hares caught secretly in snares, tarts baked in advance and cooked in the baker's oven, freshwater crayfish from the valley, snails, gigots of lamb, hams, hot sausages, *gratinées* and so many good things that the wom-

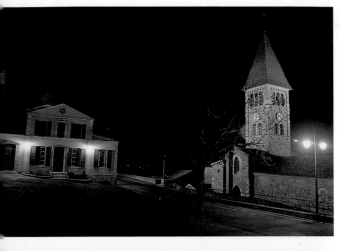

en take it in turns at the kitchen stoves. Between neighbors, that is all they talk about."

I stood in the square under the starlit January sky and imagined the festivities at Clochemerle: the inhabitants coming out of their houses, gathering to watch the torch-lit procession by the local fire brigade, the stage set with the musicians and dancing, *le bal de nuit,* the wine fountain of barrels rolled out by the municipality with volunteers spraying the barrels to keep them cool. "Everyone has the right to drink at his or her discretion. Drink as they know how to drink in Clochemerle, dance as they dance in every French country square, without paying excessive attention to the beat of the music, without useless gestures."

Gabriel Chevalier knew his Beaujolais. He was born in Lyon, studied painting at the city's Beaux-Arts, fought in the First World War and was wounded, went into business, and finally became a writer. In his chronicle of a village, the descriptive passages of the Beaujolais countryside are the work of a painter.

A mist soon spread across the square, heightening the effect of the *pierres dorées,* the golden stones, in the lamplight. At four hundred meters altitude, hill mists often hang over Vaux. I had been invited by the mayor of Vaux, Monsieur Philibert, who also owned the café, to join him and a band of winegrowers in the village's underground cellars. In that perennial *joie de vivre,* they poured me their Beaujolais, the all-weather wine, and we tasted and talked late into the night.

I do not know where Clochemerle ends and becomes again Vaux. Clochemerle, where the good humor comes from the wine of Beaujolais, where your intelligence is measured according to the finesse of your palate, where, as one old winegrower asked me that night: Surely, we have the right to dream?

"They live in this land," wrote Chevalier, "in an atmosphere of peace, concord and joy, because Beaujolais is one special wine that has never done harm. The more one drinks it, the more one finds one's wife kind and gentle, one's friends faithful, the future encouraging, and humanity bearable."

Bibliography

Arizzoli-Clementel, Pierre. *La Musée Historique des Tissus de Lyon.* Paris: Albin-Michel, 1990.

Arlott, John and Christopher Fielden. *Burgundy Vines and Wines.* London: Quartet Books, 1978.

Aulas, Michel. *Le Beaujolais à Voir et à Boire.* Lyon: Editions Xavier Lejeune, 1992.

Benoit, Felix, and Henry Clos-Jouve. *Le Beaujolais Secret et Gourmand.* Paris: Editions Solar, 1973.

Bespaloff, Alexis revised by. *Schoonmaker Encyclopedia of Wine.* New York: Wm. Morrow, 1988.

Bocuse, Paul. *Paul Bocuse's French Cooking.* New York: Pantheon, 1976.

Bocuse, Paul. *Bocuse's French Regional Cooking.* New York: Abbeville, 1991.

Bruyas, Jacques. *Le Beaujolais.* Lyon: Editions Signe Noir, 1982.

Charlet, Louise. *Tandis Que la Grille Se Referme.* Paris: La Pensée Universelle, 1988.

Chevalier, Gabriel. *Clochemerle.* Paris: Livre de la Poche, 1991.

Elwing, Henri. *Georges Duboeuf: Beaujolais Vu du Citoyen.* Paris: Editions Jean-Claude Lattes, 1989.

Fallet, René. *Le Beaujolais Est Arrivé.* Paris: Denoel, 1975.

Frangin, Bernard. *Le Guide du Beaujolais.* Lyon: La Manufacture, 1989.

Grancher, Marcel. *Quand la Soif S'Apaise...Souvenirs Gastronomiques.* Paris: Editions Rabelais, 1962.

Guillermet, Jean. *Les Savoureux Almanachs du Beaujolais.* Editions du Cuvier, 1932.

Jacquemont, Guy and Paul Mereaud. *Le Grand Livre du Beaujolais.* Paris: Editions du Chène, 1985.

Johnson, Hugh. *World Atlas of Wines.* New York: Simon & Schuster, 1971.

Johnson, Hugh. *Vintage.* New York: Simon & Schuster, 1990.

Lichine, Alexis and William E. Massee. *The Wines of France.* New York: Alfred A. Knopf, 1951.

Lichine, Alexis. *Guide to the Wines & Vineyards of France.* New York: Alfred A. Knopf, 1979.

Lichine, Alexis. *New Encyclopedia of Wines.* New York: Alfred A. Knopf, 1984.

Moreau, Roger. *Les Secrets de la Mère Brazier.* Paris: Editions Solar/Presses de la Cité, 1992.

Pivot, Bernard. *Beaujolaises.* Paris: Editions du Chène, 1978.

Richardot, J.P. *Papa Brechard Vigneron de Beaujolais.* Paris: Editions Stock, 1978.

Thomas, Georgette and François Lepraz. *Il Etait Une Fois le Beaujolais.* Paris: France-Empire, 1985.

Vermorel, Victor. *Les Vins du Beaujolais.* Dijon: Librairie H. Armand, 1992.

Vermorel, Victor. *L'Ampelographie.* Marseille: Editions Jeanne Laffitte, 1992.

Vurpas, Anne-Marie and Claude Michel. *Dictionnaire du Français Regional du Beaujolais.* Paris: Editions Bonneton, 1992.

ACKNOWLEDGMENTS

COMTE Henri de Rambuteau, *Château des Granges, Le Breuil; Président, Compagnons du Beaujolais (1974-1991)*

Louis Brechard, *Viticulteur, Chamelet*

André Vernus, *à St. Etienne-la-Varenne Vice-Président, Amicale des Beaujolais-Villages*

Jean Dutraive, *Proprietaire, Domaine de la Grand Cour, Fleurie;*

Robert Felizzatto, *Négociant, Caves de Champclos, Belleville; Président, Union des Maisons de Vins du Beaujolais et du Maconnais*

Alain Michaud, *Viticulteur, Beauvoir, St. Lager; Président, Cuvage de Brouilly*

Claude Geoffray, *Château Thivin; Président, Côte de Brouilly*

Jean-Paul Ruet, *Domaine Ruet; Président, Crus de Brouilly*

Guy Brac de la Perrière, *Château des Tours, St. Etienne-la-Varenne*

Maurice Bonnetain, *Président, Amis de Brouilly*

Olivier Ravier, *Domaine de la Pierre Bleu, Odenas*

Jean-Paul Rampon, *Caveau des Deux Clochers; Président, Crus du Regnié*

Paul Collanges, *Président, Villié-Morgon*

Andre Pelletier, *Président, Crus du Juliénas*

Jean-Paul Thorin, *Négociant, Maison Thorin; Président, Cru du Moulin-à-Vent*

Aime Bataillard, *Domaine de Belleverne; Président, Cru du Chenas*

Raymond Philibert, *mayor, Vaux-en-Beaujolais*

COMTESSE Irline de Rambuteau, *Proprietaire, Château des Granges, Le Breuil*

MARQUISE Nicole Roussy de Salles, *Proprietaire, Château de la Chaise, Brouilly*

COMTE and COMTESSE Durieu de Lacarelle, *Proprietaires, Château de Lacarelle, St. Etienne-des-Ouillières*

Louis and Jean Tête, *Négociants, Beaujeu*

Georges and Frank Dubœuf, *Négociants, Romanèche-Thorins*

Georges and François Paquet, *Négociants, Le Perréon*

Paul Beaudet, *Négociant, Pontanevaux*

Maison Champclos, *Négociants, Belleville*

Pierre Ferraud, *Négociant, Belleville*

Sylvain and Henri Fessy, *Négociants, St. Jean d'Ardieres*

Robert Sarrau, *Négociant, Romanèche-Thorins*

Jean-Louis Foillard, *Négociant, St. Georges-de-Reneins*

Herve Dupond, *Négociant, Graves-sur-Anse*

Jean-Marc Aujoux, *Négociants, St. Georges-de-Reneins*

André Gagey, *Négociant, Maison Jadot, Beaune*

Olivier Maufoux, *Négociant, Prosper Maufoux, Beaune*

Louis Latour, *Négociant, Beaune*

Robert Drouhin, *Négociant, Beaune*

Alberic Bichot, *Négociant, Beaune*

Armand Cottin, *Labouré Roi, Négociant, Beaune*

Maison Selles, *Négociants, Blacé*

Maison Collin-Bourrisset, *Négociants, Crêches sur Saône*

Johannes Papillon, *Viticulteur, St. Laurent-d'Oignt*

Denis Chastel-Sauzet, *Domaine du Moulin-à-Vent*

MADAME Flornoy, *Proprietaire, Château du Moulin-à-Vent*

MADAME Vve Louis Dailly, *Proprietaire, à St. Amour*

Claude de Rambuteau, *Château des Granges, Le Breuil*

Thierry Canard, *Domaine Blaceret-Roy, St. Etienne-des-Oullières*
Pascal Dufaitre, *Château de Pizay, St. Jean-d'Ardieres*
Raymond Mathelin, *Proprietaire, Domaine de Sandar; Directeur,*
    École de Dégustation des Pierres Dorées à Chessy
Jacques Nove-Josserand, *Président, Cave Cooperative, Bully*
Gerard and Jacqueline Trichard, *Le Bel Avenir, La Chapelle de Guinchay*
René and Christian Gaec Miolane, *Le Cellier, Salles Arbuissonas*
Pierre Charmets, *Viticulteur, Vignobles de la Rouze, Le Breuil*
George Subrin, *Viticulteur, St. Pierre sur Morance*
Yves Mathieu, *Viticulteur, Mont Joli, Blace*
Jean de Saint Charles, *Viticulteur, St. Etienne-La-Varenne*
Guy Depardon, *Viticulteur, Le Point du Jour, Fleurie*
Jean Descombes, *Viticulteur, Villié-Morgon*
Daniele Sarrazin, *Courtier, St. Laurent d'Oignt*
Michel Brun, *Maison Dubœuf, Romanèche-Thorins*
MADAME Mick Micheyl, *Montmerle*
MADAME Maryse Durhone, *Maire de Beaujeu*
Paul Bocuse, *Restaurant Paul Bocuse, Collanges-au-Mont d'Or*
René Besson, *"Bobosse," Charcutier, Vaux-en-Beaujolais*
Renée Richard, *Fromagère, Marche Les Halles de Lyon*
Jean-Paul and Fabienne Lacombe, *Restaurant Leon de Lyon*
Anne-Marie Brazier, *La Mère Brazier, Lyon*
Gilbert and Bernadette Roman, *Hostellerie St. Vincent, Salles*
Henry Marchetti, *Hôtel Plaisance, Villefranche*
Daniel Lobjoie, *Directeur, Château de Pizay, St. Jean d'Ardieres*
Claude Chevennot, *Restaurant Le Coq au Vin, Juliénas*

Jacques Mayancon, *Restaurant du Beaujolais, Blaceret*
Georges Lagarde, *Auberge de Clochemerle, Vaux-en-Beaujolais*
Christian and Sylvie Mabeau, *Restaurant Christian Mabeau, Odenas*
Robert Viallet, *La Terasse des Beaujolais, Pommiers*
Guy Fauvin, *Restaurant Les Maritonnes, Romanèche-Thorins*
Martine and Jacques Rongeat, *La Ferme du Poulet, Villefranche*
Jany-Joel and Dominique Cancela, *Restaurant Anne de Beaujeu, Beaujeu*
Yves Gudefin, *Hôtel de France, Bois-d'Oingt*
Maison des Beaujolais, *St. Jean-d'Ardieres*
Louis Prin, *Restaurant Ma Bourgogne, Paris; Académie Rabelais*
Pierre Arizzoli-Clementel, *Conservateur-Général, Musée de Tissus, Lyon*
Jean Combier, *Centre National de la Recherche, Romanèche*
Imprimerie Chevenot, *Belleville*
Françoise Texier, *Bibliothèque Municipale, Villefranche*
Robert Grange, *Mont Brouilly, Odenas*
Patrick Perche, *Photographer, Villefranche*

UNION INTERPROFESSIONNELLE DES VINS DU BEAUJOLAIS
Gerard Canard, *Directeur; Président, Compagnons de Beaujolais;*
    Proprietaire, St.-Etienne-des-Oullières et Le Perréon
Jean Chevalier, *Président*
André Rebut, *Président d'honneur*
Michel Rougier, *Délégué-Général*
Michel Deflache, *Directeur-Délégué; Proprietaire, St. Loup*
André Moiroud, *Directeur Technique; Proprietaire, Emeringes*
Monique Thirial and Yolande Chatelus